SIXTH FORM COLLEGE

This book must be returned on or before the above date.
Fines will be charged on all overdue items.
This item may be renewed twice:
Marple: 0161 484 6625 Cheadle: 0161 486 4619

Country Pottery

THE TRADITIONAL EARTHENWARE

OF BRITAIN

Country Pottery

THE TRADITIONAL EARTHENWARE
OF BRITAIN

Andrew McGarva

A & C BLACK • LONDON

This book is dedicated to all makers of pots and pans;
past, present and future.

Contents

First published in Great Britain 2000
A & C Black (Publishers) Limited
35 Bedford Row
London WC1R 4JH

ISBN 0-7136-4813-9

A CIP catalogue record for this book is available from the British Library.

Designed by Penny Mills

Cover illustrations (front): Buckley wash pan, dip pot and lidded milk jug. *Pots from the Bell-Hughes collection.*
(back): Inside of the kiln at Soil Hill Pottery, 1964. *Photograph by J. Anderson.*

Title page: Small jug from Fremington, ht. 19cm.

Frontispiece: Mesheck Sims throwing while Harold Churchill turns the wheel. Crossroads Pottery, 1930s. *Photograph from The Verwood and District Potteries Trust archive.*

Dedication page: Isaac Button throwing a large brewing-jar.

Printed in Hong Kong by Wing King Tong Co. Ltd.

Acknowledgements

FIRST, SPECIAL THANKS to Robert Fournier and John Anderson, not only for their wisdom in making their inspirational film 'Isaac Button, Country Potter', but also for allowing me to use so many of their pictures in this book. Thanks are due to the many people who have contributed; to Mick and Sheila Casson for their support in various ways, to all the potters in Chapter 12 and all the others who have been so generous and helpful. These include David and Margaret Frith, Terry and Bev Bell-Hughes, Adrian Childs and Sheila Tyler, Andrew Holloway, Mary Wondrausch, Mark and Sarah Griffiths, Duncan White, Fred Whitbread, Josie Walter, Murray Fieldhouse and Jack Doherty.

Thanks also to Reg Lloyd for access to his collection and archive, to Henry E. Kelly for his help on Scottish potteries, H. Bateson of Burton in Lonsdale, Barbara Blenkinship, Jean and Leon Morton, John Colton of the Friends of Soil Hill Pottery, Clive Daniels of Verwood Historical Society, Penny Copland-Griffiths of the Verwood & District Potteries Trust, and Islwyn Watkins, dealer in country pots in Knighton, Powys.

My gratitude also to Kathy Niblett at Stoke-on-Trent City Museum, David Dawson at Taunton Museum, Christine Stevens at St Fagans, Guy L. Baxter at the Rural History Centre, Reading, Kathryn Pryor of Norfolk Studies, and Philip Bye at East Sussex archives.

And for their sound advice and help, thanks to Linda Lambert and Alison Stace at A & C Black.

Preface

WHEN HANS COPER visited the Studio-Pottery course at Harrow during the late 1960s he found all the students were watching a film. On hearing that it was the Isaac Button film he asked why on earth they wanted him to talk to the students, 'when they had been watching a real potter'. I think that most potters believe that no matter what kind of pots they themselves make, their roots belong with the country potters who made simple functional pots for everyday life.

Our age is rightly concerned with archives, with the preservation of material about the past collected if at all possible from the last practitioners of their skills and disciplines. Andrew McGarva's generation is the last to have seen the remnants of this pottery tradition (as well incidentally, the last to know the pioneers of the modern movement – Bernard Leach and Michael Cardew). Andrew's life-long interest in vernacular styles extends to all forms, from rural architecture to functional blown glass, from weaving to traditional furniture. Moreover his own pots stem from the peasant traditions of Europe. Whether you look at his sturdy wood-fired stoneware or his large earthenware flowerpots, his complete understanding of the sources of his craft is evident.

This book is about the skills of these traditional potters and delves deeply into the practices they used. It is recounted in great detail, relating at times the minutiae of workshop procedures: lengths of ware boards for carrying pots, the number of fingers used to grab a snatch of clay for throwing. He describes in a way only a potter could the various 'holds' for throwing and the different methods of using slips and glazes.

Together with the invaluable assistance of the many photographs, always informative and at times delightful, the book is a tribute to tacit knowledge; that conduit by which ways of doing things with materials and processes are conveyed across time and space. This is the potters' heritage.

Michael Casson
February 1999

Introduction

BRITAIN HAS A HIDDEN treasure, a vernacular tradition of pottery for home, farm and garden. The pots are simple and in their way beautiful. There is no national collection, and there are few books on the subject. Museum collections – even local to where the pots were made – tend to be poor. Even today good examples can be found in local junk shops and salerooms. For a long time potters have appreciated their qualities, and most of the examples photographed in this book are owned by potters or from the collections of a small band of enthusiasts rather than public collections. What are these pots? How were they made? What was it like in traditional pottery workshops?

The long drying room at Soil Hill, 1962. *Photograph by Robert Fournier.*

Pancheons, typical of the north of England, with their white-slipped interior and unglazed exterior. The large 'wash pan' is 59cm in diameter, while the mixing bowl with a finger-wipe round the inner rim (to give a contrasting band) is only 32cm in diameter.

When Reginald C. Haggar wrote his book in 1950 *English Country Pottery* there was hardly a hand-made pot in the whole book. Since then, however, the expression has come to describe traditional pots, that is, the once common earthenware made in small potteries throughout Britain. In spite of this title these pots were not necessarily made or used in a rural setting; it is only with hindsight that we see them as part of a 'country' or peasant lifestyle. The 1965 film 'Isaac Button, Country Potter' by Robert Fournier and John Anderson, and later the Peter Brears book of 1971, *The English Country Pottery*, both helped define what was meant by the expression.

The common red clays that these potters used was dug on site. Still relatively fragile and porous when fired to 1000°C (1832°F), it was best suited for pots of generous proportions; horticultural ware, jugs with rounded rims, or thickly-made pancheon bowls for washing or bread-making (see above). Decoration was kept to the minimum, a band or two of a contrasting slip, or a lining of a light coloured slip to appeal to a public who already associated whiteness with cleanliness. Small potteries were able to provide wares not catered for by industry, and if there were a few drips from the jug, or liquids soaked into the unglazed exterior of a dish, this was of no importance within the context in which they were used. These 'simple'

earthenware pots, made with great economy, were a continuation of a production which was established in the Middle Ages.

Before the development of industrially produced pots in the mid-18th century, and improved transport links which came along at about the same time, small family-run potteries became established wherever clay, fuel and a market coincided. There was therefore a concentration of pottery works in the west of Britain, in order to benefit from the trade with the colonies. There was quite a variation in these works, some were brickyards which made chimney pots, horticultural wares and various other pots, while others were established as potteries, which then found they had a demand for drainage pipes and roof tiles.

Despite the increasing availability of factory wares, they could continue this mixed economy, particularly in more remote areas. But decline in trade was inevitable, and with more potteries closing than opening, there were only about a hundred left by the end of the 19th century. By this time there was further competition from other materials, with the development of moulded glass, enamelled pressed steel and, later, galvanised steel. Water supplies started to be plumbed in to homes and as the 20th century progressed, lifestyles changed, with progressively less home baking, cheese-making and brewing. By the end of the Second World War there were only a dozen or so traditional potteries left. Some survived by concentrating on brick and tile production, while others limited production to land drainage pipes, chimney pots and horticultural wares.

Of course, decorative wares were always made as an adjunct to normal production: one thinks of North Devon harvest jugs, as well as toy chests of drawers and rocking chairs, money boxes and so on. There was a fashion for decorative wares between 1880 and the 1920s depression, encouraged by the Arts and Crafts movement. This arrested the decline of some potteries for a while. As well as various brightly-coloured 'art ware', much 'rustic ware' was produced in this period: flowerpots and tobacco jars decorated to resemble logs of wood. This was never supposed to be great art, but because of its decorative nature these pieces tended to stay on the family shelf or dresser rather than being used, broken and thrown away. Museums and

(ABOVE) The team at Hayes Pottery, Buckley *c.* 1910, with Mr. Hayes central holding a candlestick and rustic tobacco jar. The others hold furniture supports and a large barm (yeast) pot. The stock of black-glazed milk pots await customers, a freshly made one on the board in front of the thrower, on the ground some jugs and small bowls. The team is typical of such potteries; two throwers, each with an assistant 'passer', one man to glaze, and another to handle and finish. For some jobs they all worked together; digging clay, setting, firing, and unpacking the 14 ft dia. down-draught kiln. The chimney stack can be faintly seen behind the workshop, near the apex. Firings, which held eight tons of ware took place once a month. *Photograph from Flintshire County Archives.*

(TOP RIGHT) Buckley 'hen and chickens' money pot; agate ware with applied modelling and slip-trailing. Similar ones were also made in Yorkshire. *Pots from the Bell-Hughes collection.*

(RIGHT) Some of the range of Buckley slip-banded wares; a big four-handled bread pot, wash pan, stew pots, and lading or dip pots. *Pots from the Bell-Hughes collection.*

private collections are often full of this material (sometimes of questionable taste), and much less of the plain functional ware. It is not by this decorative ware that the country potters' work should be judged. For a historian or anthropologist, they may seem more interesting, and a certain rustic charm in this decorative ware is undeniable. But any potter can see that what these old potters made best, with skill and spontaneity, were the 'ordinary' pots for everyday use. Through their simplicity and directness, they represent a honed tradition of functionalism: design of the kind where nothing superfluous exists. Plain pots have a tendency to be valued only when sufficiently distanced in time,

place of origin or rarity. A continuation of tradition is less noticed than innovation or change. The status of these cheap and unpretentious pots therefore remains low.

If we take the term 'country' to distinguish these wares from the alternative urban industrial wares, this also provides us with the time-span of our story; from the beginning of the industrial revolution in the mid-18th century up to the Second World War (although, as we will see, some of the potteries survived a little longer). These pots are artefacts from a way of life which no longer exists. Each cottager would keep some animals and poultry, as well as producing fruit and vegetables which needed

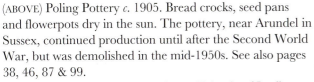

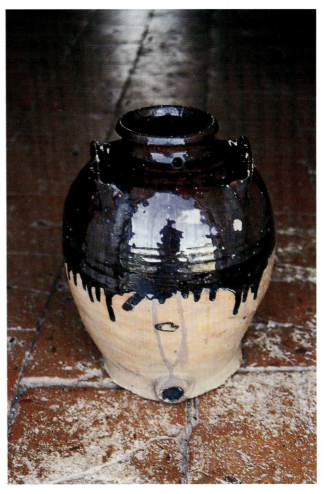

(ABOVE) Poling Pottery *c.* 1905. Bread crocks, seed pans and flowerpots dry in the sun. The pottery, near Arundel in Sussex, continued production until after the Second World War, but was demolished in the mid-1950s. See also pages 38, 46, 87 & 99.
Photograph from the Rural History Centre, University of Reading.

(TOP RIGHT) Fremington oval baking dishes, with their distinctive combed decoration through white slip, one of the items made with a special mixture of clay and river sand.

(RIGHT) Spiggot jar (used for brewing beer) from south Wales, with pale clay body and manganese slip to darken the glaze. (Ht. 33cm).

The courtyard at Wrecclesham in the late 1970s, with stacks of Fred's small flowerpots on the left, and some of Reg's larger decorative pots on the right. With the red brick buildings, one felt surrounded by red clay.

preserving and storing to last the winter. Few people moved far from their village, and accents were local as was the style of cooking. Since transport was expensive, houses, baskets, carts, furniture and pots all had their own distinctly regional style. They were made of whatever material was locally available, by people who learned their craft from older members of their own family.

This kind of pottery is often dismissed as 'common redware' or 'coarse ware'. If it was once common, surely this is a measure of its success. If it was red or coarse in comparison with industrial china, perhaps it was more suited for its purpose. The clay for some pots was deliberately made coarse by adding sand, this gave increased resistance to thermal shock and thus made them better for cooking. Pancheons and milk pots were made deliberately thick and sturdy to withstand the knocks and wear of the farmhouse kitchen and the flagstoned floor of the dairy. While various types of 'fine' wares e.g. Delftware, white salt-glaze etc. came and went, the native tradition of common pottery outlasted them all.

The introduction of stoneware to Britain came with the industrial age. In the absence of methods of mass production of glass bottles and drinking vessels, stoneware manufacture was a cheap way of making relatively thin and durable

functional ware. Soon the design of these pots were made hard-edged and machine-smoothed; here examples might include salt-glazed mugs with sprigged decoration, or the later typical spirit flagon, with straight walls in pale 'Bristol' glaze, and a brown glaze on the shoulder. These are industrial pots made by hand, even if some of the centres of production of such wares (like Burton in Lonsdale) were also home to 'country' earthenware potteries. Some potteries, like Greta Bank and Bridge End Potteries in Burton converted from earthenware to stoneware production.

The country potters used less refined and more commonly available materials and were able to fire to a lower temperature. Their glaze was made with lead in one form or another. Their kilns were round in plan, the wares cheap and seldom marked with the maker's name. By their nature heavy, it was uneconomical to transport them very far. Even today old pots tend to turn up near their place of origin.

What constitutes a 'country pottery' is a fairly subjective thing: different people have their own definitions. The childhood visits that Michael Cardew made to Fremington provided him with a nostalgic ideal which remained with him all his life. Anyone who has experienced visiting a similar pottery can empathise; one is struck by the simplicity of the process and humbled by the integrity of the work. The only evidence left of most of such country potteries is the dwindling number of surviving pots. As we can see from the map (see p. 110) they were to be found throughout Britain. They did need a certain density of population in order to survive and therefore they thin out in northern Scotland. There is very little to see today, although a very few pottery sites have survived (see p. 112).

In a business which relies on individual skill, the prospect of buying an expensive 'going concern' was of little interest to someone starting up with limited capital. If the pottery was not taken on by the next generation of a potter's family, it was usually demolished or used for another purpose.

For myself, like many others in Britain, the initial introduction to traditional earthenware making was through seeing the film 'Isaac Button, Country Potter', which showed one of the last traditional potteries in Yorkshire. When a student in the late 1970s, I was able to witness at firsthand the work of Fred Whitbread and Reg Harris at Farnham Potteries at Wrecclesham, where they continued flowerpot production in the delapidated Victorian works.

Amongst the books on the subject (see bibliography, p. 127) one of the most detailed is the autobiography of William Fishley Holland *Fifty Years a Potter*.

Apart from describing his long career, and how he gave the young Michael Cardew his first throwing lessons in 1921, the book describes Fishley Holland's apprenticeship at the family pottery in north Devon, at Fremington Pottery.

Both Fremington and the nearby Bideford potteries ended production with the coming of the First World War; to visit Fremington in those days must have been in its way idyllic, as Mr Holland describes. The buildings were of ochre coloured cob, with home-made bricks round doors and windows and pan-tiled roofs; a vine trailed around the sheltered courtyard walls, while chickens pecked below the racks where wareboards of freshly thrown pots glistened in the sun. The sculptor Henry Moore used to reminisce about the pottery in Castleford where he would go as a boy to get clay; the same pottery, Carder Bros., where the Burton in Lonsdale potter Richard Bateson was sent to work by the government scheme, the

Cutting off a flowerpot at Sutton Pottery, Macclesfield. *Photograph from Rural History Centre, University of Reading.*

Direction of Labour, for a couple of years at the end of the Second World War.

The 20th century was one that saw great changes, with the two world wars, and the economic depression that came between them. Potteries that survived until the 1960s, often linked with local horticultural industries, were closed after the introduction of plastic flowerpots; Colliers of Reading, Tuck's Pottery of Upshire, Essex, and Seaton Pottery in Aberdeen were among potteries that closed. There was also a change in attitudes to work at this time, so that Mr Button at Soil Hill could find no one to train or take on the business. The Crossroads Pottery at Verwood succumbed a little earlier in 1952; it had been the only one of several in the area to survive into the 20th century. Sons were no longer obliged to continue the family business in the changing cultural and economic environment.

At Buckley in Flintshire, north Wales, which had been a major centre of production, there were only nine potteries left by 1886 and by the 1930s there was only Lamb's and Hayes Potteries left, and these both ceased production with the Second World War.

Amongst the books mentioned in the bibliography (p. 127) apart from those cited above, some are of particular interest. *The English Country Pottery, Its History and Techniques* by Peter Brears includes a gazetteer listing almost all the country potteries in England, with a short history of each. *Made in England* by Dorothy Hartley gives a charming description of pottery-making in the 1930s in Buckley, within a wide-ranging book describing many traditional crafts. *A Family Business, The Story of a Pottery* by Peter Brannam gives an insider's picture of the development of the Barnstaple pottery factory. *Verwood and District Potteries, a Dorset Industry* by David Algar, Antony Light, and Penny Copland-Griffiths, and Mrs Copland's most recent *Pottery* in a series entitled 'Discover Dorset', give a full description of the Crossroads Pottery at Verwood among others. *The Ewenny Potteries* by J. M. Lewis was the source of much useful information, particularly on the two longest surviving potteries there, Claypits Pottery and the Ewenny Pottery. *A Pioneer Potter*, the autobiography of Michael Cardew, is full of wonderful details about Truro, Fremlington, Verwood and Winchcombe Potteries. *Making Pottery* by John Anderson is a small format picture book which shows Isaac Button at work. Some of the photographs also appear in this book, as well as stills from the film John Anderson made with Robert Fournier 'Isaac Button, Country Potter', first released in 1965.

This book is by no means a record of the histories of all the various potteries in Britain. By studying the pots from a limited number of those potteries which survived longer, or had more written about them, and the tools and methods used in their production, one can picture their ways of working and how the tradition developed. There are no Irish potteries included, and information on the few Scottish potteries has proved hard to come by. The era of the country potters is over and very few of them are still alive, but as we will see in Chapter 12 there are potters working today who in their own way continue the spirit of the traditional country potter.

CHAPTER ONE

The Wares

ONLY BY STUDYING the pots from a particular region or individual pottery can one recognise the variations in style, colour, form and texture specific to them. The pots can sometimes be found in local museums or near their place of origin in auction sales, junk shops and, increasingly, in antique shops.

Inevitably incomplete, this chapter gives a general guide to regional variations which might give clues on which to base further local research.

It is important to remember that all the old country potteries also produced bricks, tiles and land-drainage pipes. Some brickworks which employed a thrower to make chimneypots, developed this side of the business and sometimes set up a separate pottery within the works. This was the case at Colliers of Reading and there was a similar set-up at Devizes. Often the distinction between potting and brick- and tile-making was less defined. Even in the medieval period, potters made

Throwing flowerpots on a small-coned Boulton wheel (see fig 4, p. 50) at Colliers of Reading in 1955. Note the tool for making the extra drainage hole hanging on a nail behind the potter. *Photograph from Rural History Centre, University of Reading.*

ridge-tiles and drains. Brick- and tile-making was also a useful way of occupying apprentices and unskilled labourers at slack times in the pottery.

Horticultural wares

Most potteries made a full range of plain flowerpots, from large to small, as well as halfpots (of shallower proportions), and pigeon nesting bowls. Then there were tall rhubarb forcers, shorter seakale forcing bells, chimneypots, seedpans and often a range of more decorative flowerpots, including strawberry pots.

Strawberry pots

The idea of these barrel-like pots, with pockets in their sides, is said to have originated in northern Spain, where they were used in the olive groves to utilise the partial shade provided by the foliage. Whatever the verity of this, they are still a popular decorative plant pot to this day. There are two ways of making them; Mr Button used both. First, and more expensively, separate small pots are thrown and, when leather-hard, cut in half and joined to the wall of the pot. The more direct method, which was also used at Wrecclesham, was to form each 'bowl' by making a lateral cut in the pot once it had stiffened a little after throwing. With wet fingers the clay above the cut is pushed in, working back and forth, then the bowl itself is pulled out, a bit like making the lip on a jug. The rim is smoothed with the skin between the first two fingers.

Pots for domestic and dairy use

Of the glazed wares, probably the most common were the large bowls known as pancheons, panshions, pans or, in Buckley, a pan-mug. Glazed only on the interior, these flaring straight-sided bowls have a broad robust rim. This made them strong and easy to grip, as well as enabling the potter to suspend them in the kiln in 'pan rings' (see photograph on p. 103), 'L' sectioned supports which economised on the space required in the kiln when firing.

In normal production, the biggest size was the 24 in. diameter 'washpan' used for laundry. Other pans had different names. At Fremington, in descending order of size, there was the washpan, the bigpan, 'caudrens' (cauldrons), widebottoms, doughpans and so on.

At Ewenny, the bigger standard sizes included: 24, 21, 19, 17, 15, 14 and 12 in. sizes. At Buckley, standard sizes descended to 10, 9 and 8 in. diameter. Tom Jenkins of Ewenny Pottery could make sixty* 15 in. and sixty 19 in. pans in a normal ten hour working day, but this was with the aid of a 'passer' who prepared the balls of clay, wired-off the pots and lifted the pans onto wareboards.

Since they were made all over Britain, it is often difficult to identify where some pancheons came from; although some are distinctive in style, others are not. Isaac Button's were an unusually dark yellow, while Wetheriggs' ones were often greenish in colour. Buckley ones came in various colours: black, brown with yellow banding and with white slip, giving a light yellow interior. These latter were of particularly sturdy proportions and ribbed straight on the exterior. Powell's of Buckley, in the 1920s, made some with flattened rims and sponged manganese decoration over the white slip; these were sold as washing bowls for use in the bedroom.

---

* The actual amount given in Jan Lewis' book *The Ewenny Potteries* is 'five dozen' of each size. However, a dozen is sometimes used to mean 'cast' (there may have only been four to the dozen).

(OPPOSITE PAGE) Strawberry pot amongst other wares in the drying room at Soil Hill. The brewing jars must have been glazed when dry. *Photograph by J. Anderson.*

(LEFT) Wrecclesham strawberry pots in the back workshop.

(ABOVE LEFT) Two tall decorated chimney pots from one of the potteries on the south coast, probably Fareham (ht. 80cm), and a rhubarb forcer, probably from Sussex (ht. 62cm).

(ABOVE) Some of the range of sizes of buckley 'pan-mugs'. The big washpan at the back is 56cm dia. while the smallest of the group in the foreground measures 22cm.

Two Buckley wash pans, each 60cm wide and 30cm high.

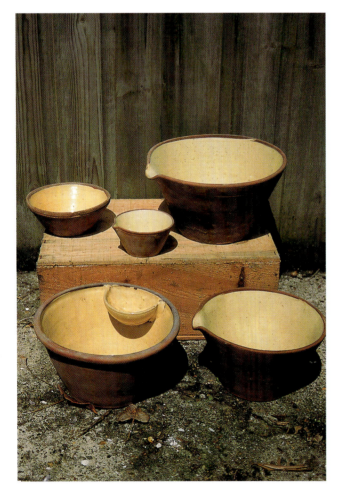

Brannam's bedroom wash pan, and various mixing bowls with pouring lip. It could be argued that from part way through the 19th century, when art ware became the main focus of the factory, it was no longer a true country pottery, and although they continued the old glazed wares, they were rather smooth 'towny' versions of the traditional pots. *Pots from the Reg Lloyd collection.*

In both south Wales and north Devon, they made washpans which were like a standard pancheon, but with an added soap dish. In the case of Brannam's ones, this was a small thrown bowl, cut in half and joined to the inner rim of the bowl, with a drainage hole in the soap dish. Sizes ranged up to 18 in. diameter. There had to be special, tall panrings made for these washpans, since the soap dishes precluded setting them in the usual way (see Chapter 11).

Pans of shallower proportions were made in various sizes for specific functions. At Truro and at the north Devon potteries, they made special pans for the making of clotted cream. These had a grogged body (sand, mica or molochite is added to the clay) and were sometimes known as 'Bodleys', after the maker of the cast-iron stove on which they were heated. The grog for these was river sand, or sometimes waste mica from the china clay pits. In order to raise the clotted cream, the pancheon full of milk was very slowly warmed, usually on top of the range, until just below boiling point. Set aside and covered with a cloth, the clots of cream would form during cooling. Another regional speciality of these potteries was the small cylindrical jars in which this clotted cream was sold.

Cream pans

Then there were the wide 'cream pans' or 'creamers'. These dishes, usually with a pouring lip, were wide and shallow. Fresh milk was put in them and the cream would easily rise to the surface and be scooped off. The example from Wetheriggs (see photograph on p. 21) is 22 in. in diameter with a depth inside of a bit less than 5 in. Standard sizes at Ewenny were 15 in. and 18 in. diameters.

Another form of dish, used for separating curds and whey, was made in the south. These were wide dishes pierced with holes. The example (on p. 21) from Fareham measures about 12 in. in diameter, by 3 in. deep, with distinctive triangular holes stabbed through with a stick. The Verwood examples have the more usual round holes. Narrower colanders were also widely produced. Fremington produced two sizes, often decorated with a spiral of slip trailing, or random drips of slip, denoting the difference between something purely functional and a pot intended for display.

Wetherigg's cream pan.

Fareham draining dish. The unglazed back of this dish is smooth with the wear and oiling it received in use in the dairy.

Verwood bread crock and peck pan. The lid of the crock, obviously fired on its rim by the flow of the rich galena glaze. The smaller pan is glazed on the interior with the more typical thin yellow glaze, from earlier days when they still prepared their own litharge. Unglazed pale exteriors showing the distinctive dark flashes of reduction. See also p. 92 and p. 93.

The Verwood potters were exceptional in that they made their distinctive upright pots instead of pancheons. They still called them pans, and they served the same functions as well as serving as a bread-crock when fitted with a lid. They did make some open bowl forms, including cream pots but, because of the way the kiln was set, it was more convenient to have upright shapes. They were made in a whole range of sizes, including bushel, peck and quart sizes.

Bread-crocks

The southern bread-crock, as made at Wrecclesham,

Lampreys of Banbury and Colliers of Reading among others, was a shape somewhere between bowl and cylinder. Sometimes they were glazed both inside and out, particularly the smaller sizes, but usually the lid was glazed only on the exterior and the pot only on the interior. This was both for reasons of economy and for ease of kiln setting. The crock would often have two small coil-like handles under the rim so that they would not get knocked, while the lid, thrown like a bowl, would usually have a pulled handle added across its cut surface.

In north Devon, they made a bread-crock of a

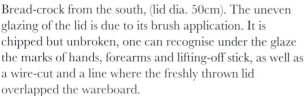

Bread-crock from the south, (lid dia. 50cm). The uneven glazing of the lid is due to its brush application. It is chipped but unbroken, one can recognise under the glaze the marks of hands, forearms and lifting-off stick, as well as a wire-cut and a line where the freshly thrown lid overlapped the wareboard.

Fremington baking dishes. These examples turned up in a box in the back of an old shop. Never used, they still had their price marked on in pencil on the exterior; 1/4 **H**d. *From the R. Lloyd collection.*

slightly taller form, with a pair of added handles on the shoulder. Smaller storage jars tended not to have these added handles, like those with an unglazed exterior for pickling eggs, or those for the storage and transport of butter, with their glazed shoulder. People used to salt butter in the summer when it was cheap and abundant, and store it for winter. In similar fashion, eggs were preserved, particularly during the Second World War, but in isinglass (sodium silicate). Many old pots still bear witness to this, with white calcium deposits on the glaze surface.

Staying with rounded forms, the bread-crocks of the north of England are tall, generously curved jars, usually with a flat lid snugly sitting in a flange inside the rim. The handles, lateral on the high shoulder, avoid being vulnerable by being placed above the shoulder and below the flaring rim. Thrown the right way up, with a thrown knob, these disc lids represent a second example of how

to make a lid that can be made directly, and finished, on the wheel. Usually unglazed, they could be inverted for firing and storage, and pierced while still soft for ventilation.

At Wetheriggs, Soil Hill, and other northern potteries, as well as this curving shape, a straight cylindric version (see photograph on p. 24) was also made. In both northern England and north Wales the stew pots (casseroles) were smaller, squatter versions of these bread-crock forms. The traditions of the two regions were linked, notably by Soil Hill Pottery which had been set up by the Catherall family, well-known potters and brickmasters of Buckley.

(OPPOSITE PAGE) Brannam's advertisement from a cookbook of 1914, showing the full range, including the distinctive crocks. *Photograph from the R. Lloyd collection.*

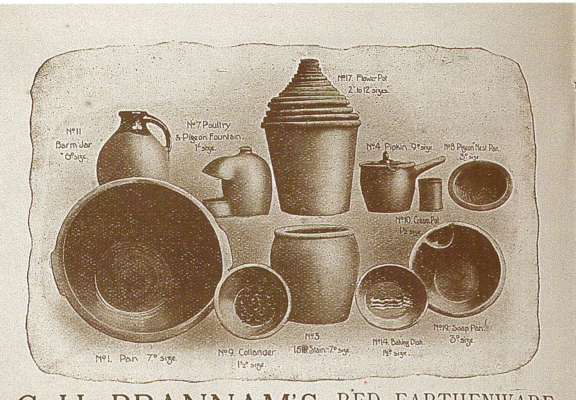

C. H. BRANNAM'S

RED EARTHENWARE
FOR HOUSEHOLD AND COOKING PURPOSES

Litchdon Pottery,
BARNSTAPLE. :: ::

DEVONSHIRE PIPKINS,
BAKING DISHES, ETC.

Mr Buttons 24lb bread-crocks in the drying room, 2nd August 1962. Note also the rouletting on the left hand flowerpot, with the pottery name and address. *Photograph by J. Anderson.*

Oval dishes and ham pans

Oval or pear-shaped ham pans were produced in many areas, especially in the south of England. (In the north they tended to make 'flesh pots', large jars, see p. 74). These were used for salting, hence the shape, which accommodated a whole ham. They were an important item in the days when killing the pig and preparing the meat to last the winter was an annual routine. They were made in north Devon, Sussex, Oxfordshire, as well as south Wales.

With flat bases and straight upright walls, they

Wetheriggs ware, with lidded bread-crock, smaller lidded stew pot, decorated salt kit, and beside it a pushed-in hen watering fountain. Central, a mixing bowl with greenish-white slipped interior, and an oval pudding dish with banded rim. The flagon behind is inscribed 'beer' into the band of white slip. *Pots from the Barbara Blenkinship collection.*

Two Brannams ham pans, with added handles at the extremities. The smaller one was made by the 'leaf' method, while the other has a separately made base. The photograph does not show the scale of these 'kieves' as they were otherwise known. The larger one is about 90cm long. *From the collection of C. Bowen.*

Pear-shaped ham pan from Sussex or Oxfordshire, perhaps from Colliers. The exterior is glazed and has similar handles to the round-sectioned ones on the jar at either end. By the similarities of glaze and handles the two pots seem to come from the same pottery. The round rims go well with the round handles.

Verwood pipkin and various bottles. Another pipkin is shown in the Brannams advertisement (see p. 23), also from the R. Lloyd collection. *Pots from the collection of R. Lloyd.*

were made either by adding the thrown wall to a separately made base, or by cutting a leaf-shape from the base of a widely thrown cylinder and rejoining the base once the pot had been pushed in, to form the required shape. Making them by this method would take four people, each with a hand on the inside and the outside of the pot.

Some of the most primitive and handsome ham pans were those made at Fremington; these get narrower towards the top and have two thick vertical handles, like jug handles. Another name for a ham pan in the west country was a 'kieve'.

A couple of variations on the cylindric forms were made at Buckley. These were made by the 'leaf' method but starting with a broad based pancheon form, producing wide bowls resembling babies' baths (see p. 107). More unusual still were those thrown like a large spiggot jar. When leather-hard, the pot was cut vertically with a knife into two halves, which were laid on their rounded sides; these would then be slightly flattened to form the bases of two matching salting pots. The cut edges became the new rims, under which handles were added, while what had been the neck of the jar provided a rest for the foot-end of the ham.

It is easy to tell by which method they have been made, as pots made by the 'leaf' method always have a line in the base where they have been rejoined, which is visible when the pots are turned over. Easy, too, to tell a pot which has been used for salting, as the clay on unglazed parts gets a distinctive pitted surface where the formation of salt crystals in the porous clay have lifted off small specks of the surface. It might seem rather alarming that brine was used with lead glaze, but salt is by definition neither acid nor alkaline, and it is acid which is a danger for lead release.

Ham pans are often labelled 'foot bath' by imaginative museum curators and antique dealers. Fremington baking dishes were similarly made by the 'leaf' method, while those from Buckley and elsewhere were pressed.

Pipkins continued to be made at some potteries, including those of north Devon and Verwood. The shape of a rounded saucepan, they had a single jutting pulled handle, a pouring lip and sometimes a lid. Designed for open-hearth cooking, they demonstrate how rustic life continued to be in some areas.

Buckley Blackwares. Tall milk pots at the rear (ht. 45cm), and a washpan with rounded edge. The smaller pan mug with flat rim and more ridged throwing on the interior is from the 18th century. The tall brewing jar, or wine jar as D. Hartley called them has a hole for a spiggot near the base. The glaze has lifted where it covered white striations of clay. For such wares the potters used two parts of 'weak' (red) clay to one of 'strong' (fireclay) which had a sandy texture, and was therefore a useful opener. In cases where the mix was not thorough enough, the refractory clay made un-intended agateware lines, on which the glaze did not properly fit. Next a bottle for beer or spirits, and a flowerpot-shaped lading or dip pot (see p. 11) and a barm pot (see p. 10).

Tall pots from Burton in Lonsdale, ht. 46cm, in both black and brown glazes. Shadows in the blushing on the brown pots rim show where the fireclay wads were placed, while drips on the rim of the other shows it was fired upside down.

Milk pots

Tall cylindrical pots, as well as a slightly convex-walled version, were a speciality of Burton in Lonsdale. They have particularly large unglazed rims. The tall milk pots from Buckley are similar, but splayed in form like a flowerpot. Sometimes lids were made for these, but usually if a lid was required it was provided by another local industry. That is to say discs of slate were used for the purpose, sometimes with a handle of wood attached but more usually without. These pots were used for storing milk in the dairy. While later pots had a smooth exterior, the older ones have a handsome ridged texture, left by the potters fingers, as he ribbed smooth the interior for easier cleaning.

A small version of this shape of pot was made but with a single vertical handle. They were used for milking or transferring milk from one pot to another. In south Wales they made similar forms, as well as tall milk pots with two high horizontal handles. Some of these had a pouring lip, and some a lining of white slip. The milk pots from Wetheriggs, by contrast, were rounded bread-crock like forms. At Fremington they made tall 'steins' which were used by the Cornish fishermen for pickling pilchards. Other jars included 'gallons', 'bussas' (or 'buzzards') and even bigger 'great-crocks'.

Smaller wares

Smaller pots included 'barm' pots for storing yeast for bread-making and home-brewing. These were cylindrical jars, about 7.5 in. in height, with a shoulder narrowing to a smaller mouth. They were made in most areas. The ones from Buckley often

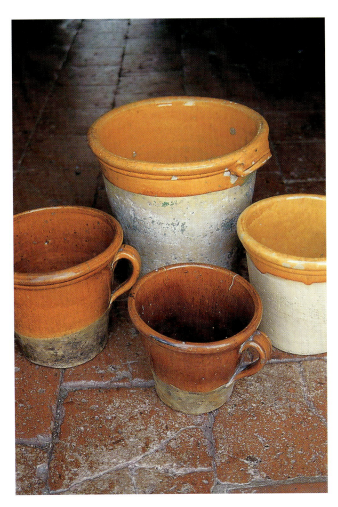

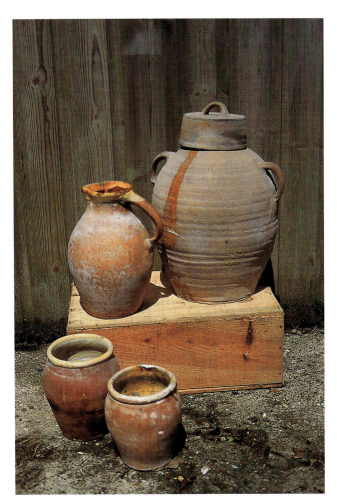

More dip pots, this time from south Wales. A manganese slip makes the bright yellow glaze a rich golden brown. Behind is a taller stein with a neat pair of handles under the rim, and a handleless pot, perhaps for lard or butter.

Fremington ware. Two simple pickling jars in the foreground with a lining of white slip, a quart jug and a handsome brewing jar made in heat-resistant sanded clay. The loose fitting cylindrical lid allows fermentation gases to belch out, while as its rim is wet no air can enter. *From the R. Lloyd collection.*

had a single handle pulled from the shoulder. One is being held by the potter on the left in the photograph on p. 10. Lard pots were of similar proportions, but tended to be simple glazed cylinders for ease of cleaning. Some potteries made chamber pots, with short swelling walls, a broad rim and single vertical handle. Often these were used for vehicles for a little toilet humour, since industry could provide cheaper, plain ones. Smaller 'gallipots' or paint pots were used for painting; usually they were made like an oversized mug. Some potteries made mugs too, as well as other small items. At Fremington they made porringers with one side handle, and a lining of white slip.

Money boxes were made at most of the potteries, sometimes fairly plain: closed-in little bottles with a simple cut slot. Others were more elaborate, with inscriptions and decorations. In Buckley and Yorkshire they made three-tiered ones with modelled hens and chickens; sometimes these incorporated a cut 'cage' section with a modelled bird within. Miniature chests of drawers and rocking chairs were made in both the above areas, and in some of the Yorkshire potteries a wide range of such items were made; cuckoo whistles, cutlery boxes, and rocking cradles for baptism gifts were just some of the more popular items.

Candlesticks were made in most places, as well as spittoons for public houses. Puzzle jugs were popular throughout Britain, although by the 19th century, fuddling cups, another pub drinking item, had fallen from popularity. In northern England and in Buckley

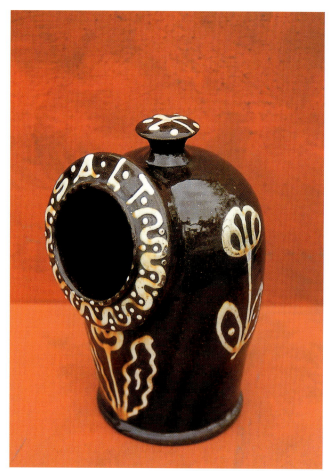

Money boxes. The one on the left with its very sharp contrast between dark body and white trailing from Cumnock in Scotland. The rich agate one is from Buckley, with the top pinched in to resemble a tricorn hat.

Saltkit also from Cumnock, or perhaps the nearby Drongan Pottery. It is easy to confuse Wetheriggs slip decorated pots with these Scottish ones, especially as the Wetheriggs ones were sold throughout the south of Scotland, but style and colour are different.
From the Mary Wondrausch collection.

supports for furniture were made, either thrown cylindrical or diabolo shaped, or press-moulded in various designs. Some were fairly plain and others more exotic, in the form of a lion's head and paws, or women's heads. Their function was to hold wooden furniture off the stone or tiled floor so that it would not get damp when the floor was washed.

Salt kits

Salt kits for storing salt and keeping it dry were confined to the north of England and Scotland. Made like a closed-in bottle, a hole is cut at the shoulder and a hood added, usually made with a separately thrown, bottomless bowl. Sometimes they are flattened at the back and a loop handle is added behind the knob, so that if required the kit can be hung up beside the stove.

Full of symbolism, the salt kit was often the vehicle for much slip-trailing, and was sometimes personalised with inscriptions. Many old examples, if not properly looked after, tended to become damaged as the porous clay of the kit becomes impregnated with salt which re-crystalises and lifts off the glazed surface.

Teapots

A similarly decorative gift item made at the above potteries, as well as at Buckley, was the teapot.

Hen drinking fountain from the West Riding of Yorkshire with thrown bowl and hood. The jar is from the north of England, perhaps Burton in Lonsdale or the north-east. Note the handles are added over the trailing.
From the collection of D. White.

Usually made to order, sometimes with two or three press-moulded spouts, they were often quite big. Like the money boxes, they were often made in 'agate-ware', that is red and white clays roughly mixed together to produce decorative striations, showing orange and brown under the iron-stained clear glaze.

Perhaps more mundanely, the hen-watering pot was a standard product of most workshops. Again like the salt kit the main part of the pot is thrown as a closed-in bottle. Sometimes this was laterally cut near the base and the section of wall pushed to form a concave shape, revealing a shallow open part from which the bird can drink. Since there is an airlock created when the pot is filled with water, it can only flow out when the water-level is reduced in the open part. It then fills to the same level, that is the surface of the dish. Sometimes there is an added handle above the open part to act as shelter. Instead of a pushed-in section, some have a hole near the base and an added drinking dish. In some of the Sussex potteries, a separate bell with a

Buckley Blackware bottle, (ht. 25cm) stewpot and early pan-mug. *From the Bell-Hughes collection.*

29

Three 'Dorset owls' from Verwood, the largest of the group, about 15cm (6 in.) high, although they were made in sizes running up to about two gallons. *From a private collection.*

hole near its rim, which sat in a separate bowl, was made. An example from Buckley has these two sections joined, giving an annular ring from which to drink. Variations are endless and are often unique to the individual pottery or potter. The principle of their function remains the same. In order to fill them, they need to be turned on their side, hole upward, and submerged in a rainwater barrel. Turned upright again, the pot is full and ready for use. Another solution to the problem of providing clean water for hens was to have a dish thrown with several parallel annular walls. When filled with water, there was a chance that not all the rings would be 'fowled' and thus would stay fit for the hens to drink. These were made at Brede in Sussex, and also in Oxfordshire among other places.

Bottles

Many varieties of bottle were made, although the stoneware potters had most of the spirits trade. At Fremington they made rounded 'costrel' bottles with two lugs with holes through on the shoulder; because of their appearance they were known as 'owls' heads'. Similarly, 'Dorset owls' were a popular product of Verwood and district. They were made in various sizes, and with a cord through the two lugs they could be slung over the shoulder and carried to work in the fields, and so be at hand when refreshment was needed. Most of the southern potteries had their versions of the 'harvest bottle'.

Larger bottles, usually with a single pulled handle on the shoulder, were made in most areas. The large bottles for brewing made in Yorkshire, like those made by Isaac Button, were equipped with a spiggot hole and a small blow-hole on the shoulder, to let the gasses from the fermenting beer escape. At Buckley, these fermentation jars were made with a wider neck and came in a great range of sizes. Made with the black glaze as well as the yellow slip banding, they may also have been used as an indoor water reservoir as an alternative to pouring from a jug. They could be replenished from the well once a day. Such spiggot pots were also made in other areas, notably in south Wales.

Brewing jar by Isaac Button. Biggest of a range of sizes, this one is about 50cm (19½ in.). *From the collection of M. Casson.*

A late Buckley spiggot pot. When your sliptrailing goes wrong, you might as well make a feature of it! *From the collection of D. White.*

Butter churns were similar, with a deep fitting lid with a hole in it to allow the passage of the stick, at the end of which were crossed paddles to agitate the milk for butter-making. One finds relatively few of these, however, as there were more practical alternatives made in other materials.

Jugs

And so to jugs, or pitchers as they are known in the United States. A standard product of most potteries, they came in all sizes from small milk jugs to enormous ones for fetching water from the well. When full, the latter were so heavy that in use they were not lifted, but tipped forward on the table. Old ones are usually worn to a smooth curve at the front of the base for this reason. At Fremington, the big two gallon ones were known as 'long toms' which cost 7 pence (before the First World War) and from this size, they descended: 5 pence for 'thirty tales' at 7 pints, 4 pence for 'gulleymouths' at 5½ pints, 3 pence for 'pinchguts' at 4 pints, 2 pence for 'tupperies' which held a quart, a penny ha'penny for 'sixties' at 1½ pints, and 'eighties' which held a pint and were otherwise known as 'penny jugs'. These north Devon jugs varied in shape from one pottery to another, but they were all roughly ovoid in form, with unglazed red clay exteriors, short necks and a dip of white slip on the rim.

The Cornish pitchers from Truro were quite different; while the Devon ones were glazed on the exterior of the rim, these are not. Entirely covered in a thin white slip to give them a pale exterior, they have a turned-over rim like a flowerpot, and a rather muscular handle joining onto the high shoulder. In north Somerset and south Wales they made high-shouldered jugs, too, but they are quite different, being glazed to the shoulder so the handle is also glazed. The pale clays of this area give the glazed part a yellowish colour, but at Ewenny,

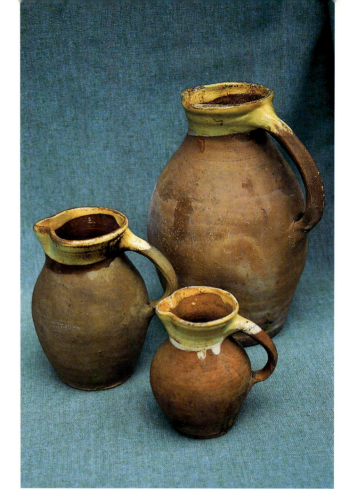

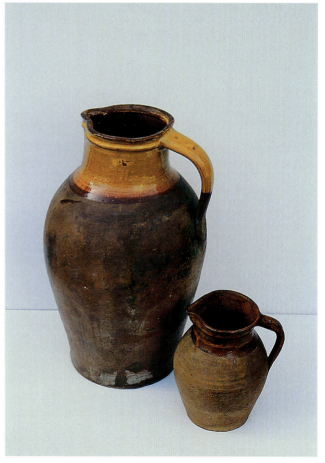

(ABOVE) Large 18th-century Buckley Blackware jug, ht. 20 in., with an extra horizontal handle at the front. *From the collection of D. White.*

(ABOVE RIGHT) Fremington jugs with their distinctive handles. *From the collection of R. Lloyd.*

(RIGHT) Ewenny jugs; see also those on p. 75 and p. 93. *From the collection of D. White.*

where they had a redder clay, they had to dip the top of the jug in white slip to achieve the effect. At Buckley a great variety of shapes were made over the years, including large round ones, taller shapes, as well as straight cylindrical ones. These tended to be glazed both inside and out. The same goes for the jugs from the north of England. Isaac Button made a range of sizes, usually with white slip on the interior, down to a tiny one with a bib of white slip on the front with 'milk' inscribed in sgrafitto.

The Verwood jugs are rather pear-shaped, glazed only on the exterior of the shoulder. One suspects this was because they had trouble with the glaze inside bubbling in the firing, but being unglazed, the water would stay cooler due to the effect of evaporation.

CHAPTER TWO

Training and Wages

APPRENTICESHIP WAS from five to eight years. The boy of 14 had to sign up for the set number of years, and agree to the master potter's conditions. In an example of an apprentice's indentures of 1882 quoted by P. Brannam (see bibliography) these conditions included: no fornication, marriage, playing of cards or dice games. Further he should 'not haunt taverns or playhouses, nor absent himself from his said master's service day or night unlawfully'. (With the hours he had to work, one wonders if he would have time for the above!) In return the lad was supplied with food and drink, lodgings, washing facilities and clothing, as well as medicine and medical care in case of illness. Wages for the first two years were 6 pence a week, rising to 8 pence for the next two years, and in his final year, 10 pence!

By the time Tom Jenkins served his apprenticeship at Ewenny starting in 1910, the boys' wages were 6 shillings per week. At the end of the 19th century at Buckley, an apprentice earned 7 shillings and 6 pence, while a thrower could earn between 36 shillings and 2 pounds; a labourer would get half that for his 12 hours a day, six days a week.

The life of an apprentice

Starting as clay-boy, the apprentice prepared the clay, weighed and made up balls for the thrower, and turned the handle or crank for the potter when he was making bigger pots. This gave the boy time to study the technique, and soon he was able to start throwing, starting on small flowerpots.

At Ewenny, work was from 8 a.m. to 7 p.m. with

a short day on Saturday, when they finished at 4 p.m. Lunch break was an hour, with a tea-break at 5 p.m. At Wetheriggs, and elsewhere, in the days of steam power, the apprentice had the added responsibility of getting steam pressure up to start the engine. They were up at 6 a.m. for this, to drive the wheels and the other machinery in the works. At Fremington work started at 6.30 a.m. with a break of half an hour at 8 a.m., lunch from 11 a.m. until 11.30 a.m. With a tea break at 1 p.m. they worked through until 6 p.m. or as early as 4.30 p.m. on dark winter afternoons. No lunch-break on Saturdays, but work stopped early at 4 p.m. Sundays were a rest day for all.

Shifts

A lot of potteries fired the kiln once a week, so in addition to the above working hours, there was night duty once a week. At Donyatt, where this was the case, one man took 6 p.m. until midnight one week, and the next worked the midnight until 6 a.m. shift. Here, normal working hours were 7 a.m. to 6 p.m. on weekdays, and 7 a.m. until 1 p.m. on Saturdays. Of course, they could always do some 'overtime' since all the throwers were paid by the 'cast' or 'ring' (as at Fremington) because there were set rates for all production.

Journeyman

Having served his apprenticeship, the potter would know how to make, glaze and fire pottery, and be able to throw proficiently up to 10 in. flowerpots. In

The team at Verwood in the 1930s. Here, as in any workshop, there was a hierarchy, with Mesheck Sims, the boss, (throwing) seconded by Bert Bailey, then Len Sims (with the board of bread-crock lids) and the lads whose main job seems to have been turning the wheels for the throwers. This one is a bevel-gear wheel (see fig. 3 on p. 49).

order to broaden his knowledge, he would become a 'journeyman' for a year or two and go, usually travelling on foot, to work at another pottery.

At Ewenny, over the years, they employed journeymen, many from Bristol, also from Winchcombe, Devizes and Bath. George Curtis of Littlethorpe Pottery was journeyman at Soil Hill. At Fremington, the young W. Fishley-Holland learned some of his throwing technique from a Staffordshire journeyman. When a journeyman himself in 1912, he was paid 21 shillings a week. Usually, after this spell away, the potters came back to the family business, or started their own, or took up employment as skilled workers. This was a healthy cross-pollenation process for these small, relatively isolated potteries. It also had the effect

of producing uniformity of style within regions of Britain.

Women in the potteries

The women of the family often dealt with the wages and accounts, as well as running the household. Sometimes, by force of circumstance, a widow would become a more active manager in the pottery. This was the case for Margaret Thorburn at Wetheriggs, who ran the pottery from the death of her husband John in 1917 until 1937. William Smith of Farnborough, in the first half of the 19th century, had his wife make out invoices, as he was illiterate. At Brannam's, already a factory at the time of the First World War, they took on women due to the shortage of labour. One of these became a thrower, while others did clay preparation, ball-making, and other jobs.

The epoch of the country pottery did not coincide with women's equality in the workplace. The potteries faded before the latter had become established. For some years, in the late 1970s and early 1980s, Elspheth Soper was thrower at Wrecclesham, but other examples are rare.

Labourers and other employees

There were other employees besides the apprentices and journeymen; many potteries had amongst their team men who did labouring jobs, also carters who also looked after the horses. Some were ball-makers, handlers and glazers, who also set the kiln. Then there was a certain amount of management and selling to be done. At Wetheriggs, labourers were hired at the annual hiring fair at Penrith, like other farm labourers. These men were taken on as 'tied' labour, on an annual basis, for 4 shillings a week and their keep (at 1890 rates of pay).

Other occasional employees were the saggar-makers, who would travel from one pottery to another making saggars, pan rings, arched and straight firebricks for kiln repairs, slabs and props. Wetheriggs pottery still has some old moulds for making pan rings, and some from Ewenny are at the Museum of Welsh Life.

Piece rates

All the throwers employed by the potteries were paid according to how much they produced; since big pots take longer to throw than small ones, a system of payment was worked out so that there was a rate of payment per 'cast', and the number of pots in a cast varied according to how quickly they could be made. A cast of pots was known by various local names; in Buckley, it was so many pots to the 'piece', while at Fremington it was so many to the 'ring'. In a cast, there would be 72 3-in. flowerpots or, for example, only six 12-in. flowerpots (see the list, p. 55). They were also sold to wholesalers by the cast, and were often therefore referred to by their cast number.

At Fremington, before the First World War, the throwers were paid 4 pence ha'penny per cast of 60 pots of the following sizes: 2½ in., 3¼ in., 4 in. and 4½ in., and this included making their own balls. A good worker could make two casts per hour, so a standard day's work was 1000 pots per day, and the pots had a retail value of a penny for three, the majority being sold to 'gentlemen's estates' as there were few private nurserymen in those days. When he was an apprentice, W. Fishley-Holland would get Bill Huxtable to throw a cast of pots in his lunch-hour, and turn the wheel for him. Then they would split the pay; a penny ha'penny for ball-making and turning the wheel, and 3 pence for throwing the pots.

By the 1920s onwards, Brannams had plenty of business with nurseries in the south-west, the Bournemouth area and south Wales. Their throwers each worked with a 'passer' who made the balls and lifted off the finished pots, and they used belt-drive power wheels. Normal production for a thrower was 1500 3½ in. flowerpots. In a week, a thrower could produce either 30,000 of the 3½ in. pots, 10,000 of the 5 in. pots, 7500 of the 6 in. pots or 1000 of the 10 in. ones. A little later, when 'jolley' machines were introduced, 4000 of the 3½ in. pots could be made in a day by one man.

Jolleying is a mechanised way of forming a pot. The plaster mould, which gives the outside profile, sits in a spinning cupped wheelhead. The inside shape is determined by a metal profile which is pivoted down onto the clay in the mould on a counter-balanced arm, after the clay has been spread in the mould with the fingers.

While a thrower at Brannams in 1920 could expect to earn 3 pounds 5 shillings per week, labourers got 1 pound 8 shillings. Production rates however were 20% lower than the firm's competitors in London and the Midlands.

Production rate, that is speed of throwing, was at its height in this sort of factory environment, often with the wheels in a row, all being driven from the same overhead shaft. Being paid by the cast, and a friendly competitiveness, both encouraged great prowess. Nowadays such cheap utilitarian wares are made by automated machines, and usually in plastic. It is no longer the role of the potter simply to produce wares in such a mechanical way, but what a good discipline it was for those lucky enough to have trained in such a workshop! (See Chapter 12, p. 112).

CHAPTER THREE

Clay Preparation

ALL THE OLD POTTERIES had good deposits of clay close at hand, usually on their own land. The geological origins of these clays are various. The Wetheriggs clay and that at Fremington are of glacial origin, while the clay at Soil Hill comes from deep sedimentary layers (see further description p. 37). Within each clay pit, there were variations in the clays, and the different qualities could be exploited by the potters to make best use of what was available. Since, in those days, transport was both difficult and expensive, and bearing in mind potters were often making brick and tile as well as large quantities of fairly thick pots, it was essential to prepare their own clay.

The claypit at Littlethorpe.

Clay winning

Usually clay digging was a summer job, when the going was easiest for the horse and cart; clay-pits can be sticky places in wet weather. It was for this reason, too, that many potteries installed narrow gauge railway tracks, e.g. Fareham, Wrecclesham, Littlethorpe and Wetheriggs. These were quite easy to install and alter or extend, as the lengths of track bolt together with their cross-pieces already fixed. On this, a tipping truck could be pushed along by one or two workers, even when filled with half a ton of clay. At Littlethorpe (see Chapter 12, p. 115) the rails descend a slight hill from the pit, before a fairly steep slope up to the works. The clay diggers, after the sweat of 'winning' the clay, could stand on the back of the clay truck, and trundle down the hill before attaching the winch cable which hauls the load up the hill to the pottery.

In the case of potteries which did not have a clay pit on site, they had to make arrangements with the local land owners, either paying an annual rent for clay-digging rights, or pay by the cartload. Some were able to dig clay on unenclosed common land, but this did not stop them getting into trouble for not refilling their clay pits. Most of the many potteries at Buckley got their clay from the Gwysaney Estate and paid once a year according to how many cart-loads had been extracted. Similarly, William Smith of Farnborough got clay from quite a distance, from Tongham or Farnham Old Park eight miles away. On the first of April each year all the local potters were summoned to Farnham Castle for a 'clay audit', to pay their year's account to the lord of the manor, the Bishop of Winchester.

In dry weather, clay becomes hard in the pit, and pick and shovel are used for clay winning. In

damper conditions, blocks can be cut out; at Wrecclesham, they used a small-bladed brick-makers' spade known as a graft, constantly dipping it in a bucket of water so that the clay did not stick to the blade. At Ewenny and Fremington clay-pits, they favoured a short rounded spade, with a 7 or 8 in. blade.

Fremington

At the Fremington clay pits, which supplied several potteries in the area, they used an interesting mining technique known as 'falling' until it was banned on safety grounds in the late 1930s. They had a big working face, like a quarry, and into this wall of clay they would dig two vertical channels, 1 ft wide, and 2 ft deep. After making a similar channel along the bottom, linking the two upright ones, holes were made at the top with long crowbars. The holes were filled with water and, after a little time and a bit more levering with the long crowbars, the whole mass would fall down, breaking into pieces ready to be shovelled into the horse-drawn railway truck. The pit is still being exploited, but now they have hydraulic diggers and tipper-lorries.

Ewenny

At the Claypits pottery at Ewenny, clay was dug each September. A years' supply could be dug and taken by wheelbarrow to the pottery in two or three weeks. Here it was stacked in the yard until required; and this was another advantage of clay winning in the summer; the action of the winter frosts helped break down the clay and improve plasticity. The finest clay from a particular seam in the clay pit was stacked separately and was reserved for making small cups, bowls and other finer pieces.

The different qualities of clay at Soil Hill and elsewhere

At Soil Hill, Isaac Button had the luxury of having several clays on site. A 48 in. band of refractory clay lies about 15 ft below the summit of the hill.

(ABOVE) Wagons and rails between claypit and pottery at Fareham, 1966. *Photograph by J. Anderson.*

(BELOW) Digging clay at Wrecclesham; Reg Harris, 1978.

Mr Button bringing the clay down from the pit in his vintage flat-bed lorry. *Photograph by R. Fournier.*

W. B. Hunt at Poling Pottery filling the second soaking pit from the heap behind him in the yard. In the foreground, the other pit is full, and covered with damp sacking. *Photograph from The Rural History Centre, University of Reading.*

Some 60 ft below this, under a 2-ft thick band of coal is the 'hard bed' of fireclay, which was used to make firebrick and kiln-furniture. Fifteen inches from the middle of this 6 ft seam is the purest clay, which was used both as white slip and in the glaze. Again 60 ft lower than this was the 'soft bed', a 4 ft band of dark coloured clay which was used for the body, which of course fired red at 1000°C (1832°F).

At Littlethorpe they use the sandy clay from the top of the pit when making big ware, and the finer clay from further down for smaller pots. At Fremington pottery, the clay was very fine, and could be used pure for small ware, and with the addition of fine sand for bigger pieces. The sand was obtained from the river bed above Bideford bridge; coarser and larger quantities were used for cooking ware, and the coarsest grade of all went for the clay for making ovens.

At both Wrecclesham and Verwood, roughly 10% sand was added to the throwing body, while at Soil Hill it occured naturally in the clay; it was simply a question of how much to sieve out. The sand helps eliminate drying cracks which sometimes occur across the base of pots, as well as cutting down the possibility of cracks in the firing.

Preparing the clay

With the clay stacked in the pottery yard, depending on the qualities of the clay supply, potters diverge into two camps for the next stage in its preparation, with roughly a north/south divide, although there were exceptions. In the northern group, which included Wetheriggs, Soil Hill and the Buckley potteries, the clay was blunged, seived and run out

Reg Harris cutting a pug of clay from the pugmill. The full soaking pit by the pugmill is in the left hand corner of the picture.

into drying pans of one sort or another. In the south, for example at the Ewenny potteries, Fremington, Dicker, Wrecclesham and the Verwood potteries, the clay was simply soaked in a brick-lined pit for a few days, remaining in the plastic state.

The soaking method

At Wrecclesham, the soaking pit is positioned near the door from the yard where clay was left to weather. At the other side of it is the old belt-driven pugmill conveniently situated for mixing the clay (see description on p. 44 –5). Once the clay had been soaked in the pit for two or three days, it was pugged, and the extruded blocks (or 'pugs') of clay were stacked in a damp corner with a covering of damp sacking. The sand was layered in with the clay in the soaking pit, so that when it was dug out it was already fairly well distributed. Having been stored for a week or two, the pugs of clay required for throwing were put through the pugmill again before a final 'knocking up' into balls.

George Bourne (Sturt) describes the process carried out in Farnborough in the 19th century (see p. 127), where the clay, once soaked, was wedged by foot rather than being passed through a pugmill.

> . . . The clay being brought home, into pits
> (two pits) in layers, with shovelfuls of sand.

Then it was well watered, and so remained for 24 hours. From the pits it was taken out in rolls and spread on the floor in one of the potshop 'houses'. There men, barefoot, trod it into little ruts picking out any stones their feet found.

At the Crossroads Pottery at Verwood they continued these same techniques until the closure of the works in 1952. Here the clay, grey-blue in colour, was soaked in a pit of about 10 ft square and 2 ft deep, before being stacked round the sides of the brick-floored lean-to clay-room. The boy would get some clay from the stack, having sprinkled some sand on the floor. The potter doing the wedging, with supporting stick in hand, rhythmically trod the soft clay flat with the right foot. When thus spread, this was rolled up into several rolls, and the process repeated. After three treadings, finding and removing any stones in the meantime, the rolls of clay were taken to the weighing-out bench, where it would be given a final hand-wedging before use.

Wedging

As well as getting rid of air bubbles, the process of wedging provided a last opportunity to pick out any stones. It is familiar to most potters, although wedging was not universally practised. A lump of clay is placed on the solidly-built wedging bench. With a wire, the clay is cut diagonally upwards from the bench, away from the potter, making two wedge shapes. Lifting the upper wedge of clay above the head, it is banged down into the other, the block turned 90° and the whole process repeated until the clay shows no variations in hardness.

Each time the clay is cut and banged together, there are twice the number of layers. There are variations in the process; using a fixed wire for example, but further kneading of the clay does not seem to have been a common practice.

The blunging method

The other method of clay preparation was to blunge it, that is to reduce it to a liquid slip by adding water and agitating the mixture. The simplest form of

Wedging at Lakes of Truro. *Photograph from the R. Lloyd collection.*

blunging, which continued to be used even in industrialised Stoke-on-Trent into the 20th century, was described by the Rev. Dionysius Lardner in 1832 in his treatise *The Cabinet Cyclopaedia*, a study of the manufacture of porcelain and glass:

> The mixing of the clay, which is called blunging, is effected in a trough five feet long, three feet wide, and two and a half feet deep. In order to fully break down the clay, and incorporate it with the water, a long wooden instrument, formed with a blade at one end and a cross handle at the other, is moved violently about the trough in all directions, so that this becomes an operation of great labour.

Although photographs exist of these 'blungers' at work – levering the long-handled tool against the solidly built trough, pulling down on the 'T' handles – the shape of the blade remains a mystery. Presumably it, too, was 'T' shaped to cut through the clay in the trough.

The first mechanisation of the process was to develop horse-powered blungers.

In Richard Warners *Second Walk through Wales* of 1798 there is a somewhat muddled description of the process, as carried on at one of the largest potteries in Buckley, probably Catherall's:

> The workmen place it in a circular cistern called a bulging (*sic*) pool, when,

whilst it is covered with water, it is kneaded by a cylindrical machine which performs a double revolution round its own axis and an upright pole in the centre, and pounds it completely. It is then tempered by boys who tread it under their naked feet for some hours, and lastly it is passed through a fine silk sieve to free it from stones and dirt.

(ABOVE) Wedging by foot at Verwood. *Photograph from The Verwood Historical Society.*

(LEFT) Len Sims wedging, *c.* 1935. The floor has been sanded from the heap on the left. The last batch he prepared is piled up on the left further back. This is the same room as the previous picture but taken from the other end. The mysterious cogged machine in front of the drying racks seems likely to be an extruder judging by the amount of gearing, and the long narrow table extending from it. *Photograph from the Rural History Centre, University of Reading.*

Claypan Soil Hill. A leak has been temporarily avoided by walling off the hole with a few bricks and some clay. *Photograph by R. Fournier.*

This intriguing description may be the result of a muddle of two machines, one a pan mill, where two upright wheels rotate about a central axis in the manner of a cider mill, and the other a blunger. Since the described machine is for crushing and indeed kneeding plastic clay, what came out would be ready for being wedged by foot, but if sieving took place, they must also have had a blunger, since sieving of the liquid slip would logically follow the blunging process.

Edward Dobson, in his *A Rudimentary Treatise on the Manufacture of Bricks and Tiles* (1850) describes, with illustrations, a large horse-powered blunger of a type used by brick-makers. This was a huge thing, 30 ft in diameter, but with a circular island in the middle, giving a ring-shaped mixing trough of 6 ft across. Two horses, harnessed in a two-horse gin, dragged a diametrically opposed pair of 'knives and harrows' round a central axis. There were smaller versions, however, as Michael Cardew discovered when he took on Becketts Pottery at Winchcombe. In the orchard there, somewhat overgrown by then, was the old mixing pond, with a brick paved circular track round it where the horse used to walk. It was linked by a short pipe to the sunpan with a little 'gate' at one end, and a metal grid where the slip entered the sunpan.

The advantage of blunging is that all roots, stones and other material is caught in the sieve, and the clay is thoroughly mixed. There is a particular advantage to the process if there is a risk of finding

Wetheriggs steam-powered blunger.

lime in the clay being used. With the big blunger at Wetheriggs, they could recover enough sand from the bottom of the blunger trough to line the sunpan. Potters working today usually line their settling pan with synthetic cloth, which keeps the clay cleaner, rather than sand. Only a thin layer of sand is picked up by the bottom surface of the clay, and this allows the clay to be lifted, when ready to be moved to the clay store. As the clay dried in the sunpan, the top surface would be ready before the bottom, so, when they could be handled, the blocks would be turned over or put on end to expose the damper parts to the air.

The mechanisation of blunging

When steam power was introduced in the potteries in the course of the 19th century, the same sort of system could be mechanised. The steam-powered

Soil Hill. The clay has been unloaded (left) on the higher ground by the top of the blunger. The drive-belts are protected from the weather by a little roof with the remains of canvas sides. The wooden gutter which takes the slip from the sieving basin to the claypan under its lean-to roof leans against the wall by the door. The stopcock outlet of the blunger can be seen at its base, between the posts of the wooden structure from which the sieve is suspended by chains. *Photograph by J. Anderson.*

blunger at Wetheriggs built in 1855 has been restored to full working order, and can be seen by visitors to the pottery. The trough of the blunger is a brick-lined pit some 14 ft in diameter, and 3 ft deep. The central axis, a large beam, has a metal frame attached across it, from which are suspended spiked harrows to break up the clay as the steam engine drives them round. By means of a lined ditch, the 'gripp', the slip was run off down to the sunpan, a level rectangle of ground 60 ft by 50 ft surrounded by a bank of earth and lined with sand recovered from the previous year's mixing. This was a spring job, the clay having been weathered over winter, from last summer's clay winning. In a day's blunging, they could cover the surface of this settling pan with about a couple of inches of slip, and the process would be continued until they had a depth of about 18 in. As evaporation occurred over the next couple of months, and slip slowly turned to workable clay, lines would be drawn in the surface, so that as it shrunk it would form blocks of a convenient size to lift.

Since large amounts of water were required for the process, the potters had to make provision. At Winchcombe, there was a pipe which brought water from further upstream in the River Isborne to the blunger. At Soil Hill they had a little reservoir further up the hill which similarly supplied a pipeline to the head of the blunger. They had the same at Wetheriggs, fed by a spring up on Clifton Moor; in addition they pumped back the water from the settling slip, and also stored rain-water in tanks, which had been collected from the roof guttering.

In most sunpans, where the slip entered, there was a small wall or trough from which the slip could overflow into the main sunpan. This ensured there was no turbulence when the wave of slip arrived down the gripp, as well as retaining the coarse grit which, being heavier, stayed in this separate compartment. The finest particles of clay travelled farther in the settling-pan, and this could be set aside for finer wares, while big-wares would be made with clay from near where the slip entered.

Further technological developments

By the end of the 19th century, technology had moved on and smaller blungers became available with hexagonal tanks made of flat cast-iron sections bolted together. These could break down the clay much faster, with several vanes or paddles radiating from the central axis.

Many such blungers are still in use, now with electric motors driving the belts rather than steam engines (see Chapter 12, potteries 10, 11 and 18). With these smaller blungers came the development of heated drying pans, which liberated the potters from having to prepare all the year's clay in one lot. At Wetheriggs, they had a heated drying pan as backup to the big sunpan. The slip was made to flow into a shallow trough made of interlocking (tongue-and-groove) fireclay slabs, which also acted as the roof of flues which passed beneath. With a fireplace at one end, and a chimney at the other, they soon had the slip steaming.

At Soil Hill, as well as at some of the potteries at Buckley, this was taken a step further, by incorporating the drying pan with the flues of the down-draught kiln (see fig. 6 on p. 64). With the drying pan under cover, the potters could prepare their clay independent of the weather. In a regular routine, clay was blunged and the drying pan filled before each firing.

An early pugmill being used (probably by brick-makers) in Norfolk photographed by the pioneering photographer P.H. Emerson in the late 19th century. *Photograph from Norfolk Studies, Norfolk County Council.*

Mixing the clay

Whether the clay was blunged, or simply soaked in a pit, the next thing was to mix it. As we have seen, in the early days, this was by foot-wedging, but in most places some form of mechanical mixer was introduced in the 19th century.

At Ewenny Pottery they had a 'clay mill' which had two horizontal rollers, each 1 foot in diameter, and 3 ft long. The bearings of one of these rollers could be adjusted to alter the gap between the two. Like the contemporary farm machinery, the original power source which turned them was provided by a spinning shaft driven by an axis connected by cog wheels, which in turn was turned by a horse trudging round its circular path. The clay was shovelled into the top of the rollers, and dropped below, three times over, each time reducing the gap from half an inch to about a quarter of an inch on the final milling. This broke up any harder clay as well as squashing the clay together. It took the clay-boy about a day to mill enough clay for a thrower's weekly supply, between

two and three tons. In the 20th century such crushing rolls were incorporated as feed rolls on some pugmills (see photograph on p. 46).

The development of pugmills

The early pugmills were vertical wooden barrelled machines, with a central axis with blades attached, angled so that they both cut the clay and pushed it towards an exit hole. The barrels of such machines were almost literally that, made of thick planks and heavy iron banding. Set up with a wooden ramp, the clay could be tipped in from the top, and the mixed and compressed clay collected as it extruded from a hole near the base. Sometimes they were set up to incorporate a soaking pit within the circular path where the horse walked (see photograph on p. 45). There were cast-iron pugmills of this design, of which there is an example at the Weald and Downland Open Air Museum (Singelton, Chichester, West Sussex).

SUSSEX POTTERY: PREPARING CLAY IN PUG

(ABOVE) Pugging at Dicker Pottery, with the soaking pit incorporated within the horse's path. One man leads the horse round, another fills the pugmill, a third takes off the lengths of extruded clay and knocks it into blocks to be transported by another with his brick-makers barrow. The long building behind is the typical shape of a drying shed for bricks and tiles, with the open sides and the boards along the sides to ensure the rain does not get in. *Photograph from the East Sussex County Council archives.*

(RIGHT) The pugmill at Soil Hill, 1961. The motor runs a large flywheel with three 'V' belts. A smaller wheel on the same axle runs a flat belt to the big drive-wheel of the pugmill which is connected to the shaft of the pugmill by cogwheels. On the floor in front of the axle block is the clay just brought in from the claypan. *Photograph by J. Anderson.*

When steam power came in, at the end of the 19th century, with 'line transmission' (horizontal shafts with drive wheels attached), it was more convenient to change to horizontal designs. Soil Hill and Littlethorpe had typical examples, the clay being fed in the top side of the cast-iron barrel, with the extruded pug of clay coming from the side at the far

end. At Wrecclesham they had a similar design, but with the extrusion coming from the end of the barrel. By contrast with the above models made by the firm Edwards and Jones, this was home-made, the barrel having been made from an old water-storage cylinder.

The coming of such machines must certainly have made the work of the potters less arduous, but it was not without its dangers. Isaac Button lost the end of his finger in an accident with the steam engine. He was fortunate in comparison to Caleb Arlidge of Donyatt, who lost a hand to a pugmill in 1912.

There were some potteries which used other variations on the 'normal' pugmill, particularly those where brick and tile was of primary importance. At Wetheriggs they had a self-lining box pugmill with, instead of a cylindrical barrel, a cast-iron box. This is similar to the one being used by Mr Hunt at Poling Pottery (see photograph), but this model, probably made between the two world wars, has the added sophistication of feeder rolls. These steel rollers crushed any harder pieces and stones, before dropping the clay into the pugmill box. As the rollers turn, knives set near their surfaces ensure the clay does not adhere but drops down. One of these knives is visible below the roller, and the extruded clay can be seen emerging at the lower level, between the two buckets. When using a spade with soft clay, a bucket of water is always within reach, to dip the spade in and thus avoid the clay sticking.

Mr. Hunt at Poling Pottery with his box pugmill. The flat belt drive-wheel can be seen behind him. *Photograph from The Rural History Centre, University of Reading.*

CHAPTER FOUR

The Potters' Tools

W E HAVE ALREADY seen the machines used in clay preparation and at this stage we come to the tools used in the making of pots. Since throwing was the primary method of production, wheels were obviously important. Once made, using various smaller tools: ribs, cutting wires etc., the pots were lifted onto wareboards, which would then be lifted and moved to drying racks. Decorating, too, needed specific tools like slip-trailers and roulettes. In this chapter, we examine these tools before looking in further detail at the processes for which they were used.

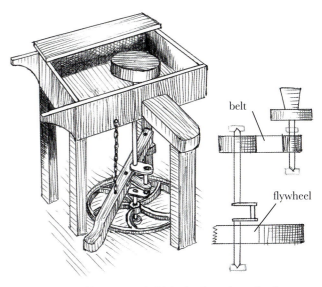

FIG 1 A typical home-made kickwheel, set into the floor and built into the wall with a window above on the right. Diagram of the workings of a geared kickwheel, like that used by Fred Whitbread.

Wheels

Whereas throughout the rest of Europe the simple momentum wheel was used to make small pots, in Britain the standard small ware wheel, at least from the mid-18th century, was the crank-shafted kickwheel. By having a crank in the axis loosely linked to a swinging suspended kick-bar or treadle, the momentum of the flywheel can be easily maintained and controlled by the continually swinging foot. The flywheel which gives this momentum has its heaviest part at the periphery. A 19th century example at Winchcombe Pottery has an ironshod wheel like a cartwheel, probably made by the local wheelwright. Another, at Ewenny Pottery, has a cast-iron flywheel off an old chaff-cutter.

Examples of these wheels can still be seen in the old potteries, where the wheel is usually solidly built into the floor as well as being fixed to the wall to avoid any movement in the frame. On these

versions, the swing end of the kick-bar is attached to the square wheel-tray, just next to the seat, giving a comfortable sideways diagonal swing; smooth running is important on a wheel where a thousand small pots might be expected to be made in a day. These kickwheels tended to be home-made, with the shaft and flywheel supplied by the local wheelwright or blacksmith, so that there is no standard model. They were made to suit the individual potter, his length of leg etc. The seat level on such wheels tends to be either at the same level as the wheel-head, or a few inches lower, to enable the potter to be in a comfortable position without bending his back.

Harold Churchill provides the motive force for Mesheck Sims to throw jugs at the Crossroads Pottery, 1930s.
Photograph from The Verwood and District Potteries Trust archive.

At Wreccclesham, Fred Whitbread used to use a geared kickwheel. It has not one, but two shafts or axels; the first with the flywheel, the crank, and a drive-wheel which by means of a flat-belt drives the secondary shaft, at the top of which is the wheel-head. The difference between the diameter of the drive-wheel on the first shaft and the smaller one on the second creates a gear ratio of roughly 2½:1. This means there are fewer kicks for more spin, good for the high speeds needed to make small pots quickly.

Throwing larger pots

Before power-driven wheels were developed, throwing larger pots meant that an assistant had to provide the motive force, while the potter concentrated on throwing. A further type of crank-shafted wheel is shown in use at Verwood (photograph above). With no flywheel to give momentum, the crank section in the shaft is enlarged to the size and proportions of a woodworker's brace and bit. A stout pole with a leather loop does the driving, while the momentum is provided by the broad wheel-head and the weight of the clay upon it. Reg Harris continued to use a wheel of this sort into the 1980s, particularly when joining sections of large pots made in two or more parts.

The 'great wheel' was another form of two-man wheel. Using a rope-drive system, the 6-ft diameter drive wheel was cranked round by a boy. Passing under a two wheeled roller, the rope, now in horizontal plane, passed below the wheel-tray to a drive-wheel on the shaft of the wheel. The boy, some 15 ft away soon got used to the speeds required; fast for centring and slow to finish. Fishley-Holland still had a great wheel after the Second World War, and one was occasionally used at Brannams into the 1950s.

With the coming of cast-iron machinery at the end of the 19th century came the last development in man-powered wheels. It can be seen in the photographs of Buckley and Verwood (see photograph on p. 34). A small bevelled gearwheel

Lamb's pottery, Buckley 1909. A bevel-gear wheel with raised seat and added cross-bar for
big ware production. *Photograph from the D. and M. Frith collection.*

on the shaft is driven by a large vertical one. This in
turn was connected to the handle in front of the
wheel-tray. At Winchcombe, Sid Tustin used to turn
such a wheel for Elijah Comfort. Sometimes he
would deliberately jolt the wheel speed, to amuse
himself and annoy old Elijah.

Belt-driven wheel

With the introduction of steam-power came belt-
driven wheels which continue to be used, even
though the source of power has changed first to
diesel engines, then to electric motors. Often, as at

FIG 2   The rope-driven 'great wheel'.
FIG 3   (RIGHT) The bevel-gear wheel.

Wrecclesham, the extravagance of power wheels was limited to one, for big-ware production, while kickwheels continued to be sufficient for smaller pots. The power wheels all had solid cast-iron frames, and were often supplied without wheel-tray or seat, so that the potter would make his own to suit himself. They were of three main types: the cone wheel, the 'disc-friction' wheel and the disc-drive wheel. These first are known after the firm which first produced them: Boultons of Burslem.

'Boulton' cone-drive wheels

The speed at which the Boulton cone-wheels run is regulated by the foot-pedal. There are two cones, one inverted; the one connected to the wheel-head is metal and slightly convex. The inverted drive-wheel is shod with leather. With the pedal at its highest, the cones are not engaged, and the wheel-head free-running. As the pedal is depressed, the narrowest part of the drive wheel engages with the widest diameter of the steel cone, giving a slow speed. As the pedal is further depressed the ratios between the diameters at the point of contact between the cones alters, so that when the pedal is fully depressed, top speed is achieved. Now the widest part of the drive cone touches the narrowest diameter on the other.

Because of their strength and the subtlety of the speed control, these were very popular wheels particularly among the makers of big ware. They came in a range of models; those with smaller cones for faster speeds and less variation in ratios, for small repetition work and those with broader cones for big pots. They were used all over Britain; at Brannams of Barnstable, Colliers of Reading, Ewenny Pottery, Littlethorpe, and at Soil Hill. Many are still in use today. Although Boultons went into liquidation in 1988, Wm. Boulton spares and machinery are still being produced by Co-bam Ltd of Burslem, to whom I am most grateful for the illustrations of the wheels.

The disc-friction wheel

The disc-friction wheel (see illustration on p. 51) has a different method of controlling the speed. This is the type of wheel used by Reg Harris, and Arthur Schofield's one is still in use at Wetheriggs today. Here, below the wheel-tray, runs a horizontal shaft with a belt-driven drive-wheel at one end, and a disc of metal at the other. On the vertical wheel shaft, which has the wheel-head at the top, there is a rubber or leather-shod driving-wheel which engages with the disc. It can be moved up or down by means of the foot-pedal, as this drive-wheel is

FIG 4 Boulton cone wheels.

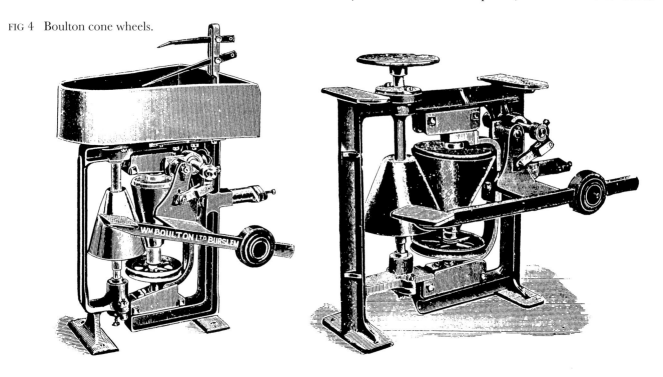

connected to the wheel shaft by means of a pin which engages with a groove in it. At the pedal's highest position, the drive-wheel is not in contact with the slightly concave surface of the disc. As it is depressed, the speed increases as the drive-wheel comes into contact with the disc, whose speed is greater at the periphory than at the centre. Various makers of these wheels made slightly different versions, but using the same mechanism; they are sometimes referred to as the 'Scotch wheel'.

The 'Armitage' wheel

Finally, the type of wheel Isaac Button used for big ware was the disc-drive or 'Armitage' wheel so called after one of the makers of this style of wheel. These too were quite widely used, at Lambs of Buckley and at Brannams for example. Like the 'Scotch' wheel, there is a low horizontal shaft with the drive-wheel at one end. It is for this reason one can see the flat-belt from the overhead line-transmission passing in front of Isaac Button's wheel-tray. Near the other end of this horizontal shaft is a leather-shod wheel. On the vertical wheel shaft, at the top of which is the wheel-head, there is a metal disc, running like the flywheel of a kickwheel, only lighter. Before depressing the foot pedal, there is no connection between the

The author at his 'Armitage' disc-drive wheel. The seat is set low for the production of small domestic ware pieces.

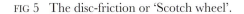

FIG 5   The disc-friction or 'Scotch wheel'.

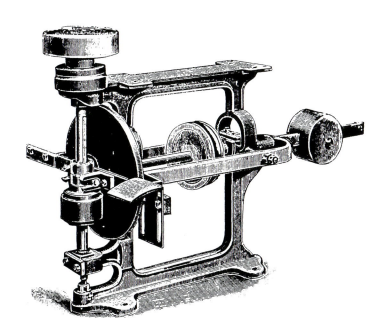

horizontal and vertical shafts, but as it is pushed down, the whole horizontal axis moves along in its bearings, and the leather wheel comes into contact with the underside of the disc, driving the wheel-head round. In practice there is not much variation in speed, it is virtually one set speed once the drive-wheel is engaged. Like the previous two types of wheel, this one has a heavy counter-balance on the foot-pedal bar which returns the mechanism to the disengaged position.

Racks and boards

Once thrown, the soft pots were lifted onto boards, which could then be carried to the racks for drying.

As can be seen from the photographs, before the

days of wheeled racking systems there were two main types of racking. Either there were stout upright poles with holes at regular intervals (e.g. every 6 in.) into which horizontal pegs could be pushed; the boards then rested on the pegs. Or the racks had heavier cross-bars onto which the potboards could be slid. This latter system was often used over heated flue systems (see Drying, Chapter 8).

The wareboards or potboards varied in length and width according to what was being made. At Verwood they had some broad ones 18 in. by 6 ft for the big bushel pans. They had 8 ft ones at Wetheriggs, and at Fremington they were 7 ft long by 1 ft wide, with enough space for 40 penny jugs. At Wrecclesham they were a bit narrower, made of two long thin planks fixed together with a lath at either end. Larger pots were transferred to slatted boards for the final stages of drying.

Tools

Apart from a wheel, clay, and water for lubrication, a few small tools were used to create a pot. Most pots would be given a smooth surface towards the end of the throwing process using a 'rib', a flat tool with a straight or curved edge. On an upright pot, the rib would be used on the exterior, while the fingers on the inside of the pot pressed the wall of the pot to the rib. It thus gave a smooth profile with fewer ridges, and also got rid of excess slip, making it possible to lift the pot once the cutting-off wire had been passed under the pot to release it from the wheel-head (see photograph on p. 15). Once ribbed smooth, sometimes a roulette was used, that is a small wheel with either a decorative pattern or printers type on the exterior surface. Held in a small handle by means of a pivot, the wheel can run freely so that when it is brought into contact with the surface of the freshly made pot, a continuous pattern or legend can be impressed (see p. 72).

Ribs

Ribs, like most of the tools, were cut by the potters themselves out of what they had available: steel cut from a worn out shovel, slate or wood. For the exterior of pots, a rectangular one, say 4 in. by 3 in. was used. For the interior of pancheons, one with rounded corners, or a 'half-moon' was needed. They did not have to be complicated to work well; usually they would have a hole made in them for grip and also for hanging them on a nail when not in use.

Most country potters did not use 'profiles', that is small ribs cut to form particular ridges or rims, although they are mentioned as having been used at Farnborough. There was however one type commonly used. This was to make a ridge at the bottom of the wall of a pot, e.g. on some 'Dorset owls' or on salt kits from Scotland. The advantage to the potter of this decorative foot ridge is that the raw pot is much easier to grip when dipping it into slip or glaze. The small rib used for this is triangular or pointed in shape with the sharp point cut back into a concavity to give the required sized beading.

Cutting-off wires

Cutting-off wires used at Wrecclesham, instead of having the usual wooden toggles at the ends, had rolls of cotton to pull on. The 'cows rib' or lifting-off stick is described later (see p. 72).

Roulettes

Roulettes were used by some potters to decorate their ware. Medium and large sized flowerpots from Donyatt, Soil Hill and some of the largest flowerpot factories e.g. Ward of Darlington and Sankey of Bulwell, Nottinghamshire had roulettes with the name and address of the pottery. Bookbinders' roulettes, pastry wheels and cogs from clocks were also used to give a decorative banding, for example on the shoulders of Fremington bread crocks, or on some of the Verwood pans. These tools, made of wood or metal, were kept in the thrower's water pot, to be wet in order to resist sticking to the ribbed surface of the freshly thrown pot. Old printers' type was sometimes used for inscription, most famously by some of the Sussex potteries, who filled the letters with white slip and, when the pot was dry, scraped the surface to give sharp definition to the printing. Type was also used in many other areas, including

Divided press-moulded dish from the north-east of England. *From the R. Lloyd collection.*

some of the Scottish potteries and some of those in the north of England, as well as north Wales, particularly on decorative presentation pieces where the lettering would simply be glazed over with a clear glaze, or be under a dip of white slip under the glaze.

Tools for slip decoration

Slip-trailers were often made out of a twisted cows horn with a goose-quill stuck into a hole made in the pointed end. It was important to get the right horn, not too big, so that it was comfortable in the hand, and twisted at a right angle, so that the quill could be held level to stop the flow with no spillage from the top. Any container would do, as long as it was reasonably small and could have a quill fixed at right angles to the container's surface. By the time Dorothy Hartley knew the Buckley potteries in the 1930s, they were using an old cocoa tin with a quill projecting from its base in at least one of the two remaining potteries, Hayes and Lamb's.

By this time, apart from more decorative pieces like baking dishes, the slip trailing used at Buckley for ordinary wares was restricted to banding, on the shoulders of stew pots and jugs, or inside the rims of pancheons. It is difficult to tell when the trailing was done, but it is likely that this was one of the jobs a 'passer' or thrower's assistant would do before the pot was removed from the wheel-head. Often the

stew pots and bread-crocks from here and from northern England have their handles applied over the continuous trailing. In northern England and Scotland, great decorative use was made of what these trailers did naturally, that is the blob, diminishing to a thinning tail. With repeats and variations it was the basis for many decorations, which perhaps reached a zenith in the dishes and salt kits of the potteries around the Newcastle area. Of course, trailing is easier on a raw body rather than a wet slip, but these pots had to be made and decorated quickly.

Another use of wet slip for decorative effect was to wipe through it to reveal the red body below. Often white-slipped pancheons have a finger wipe round the rim, giving an added emphasis. In north Devon they took this a stage further and combed wavey lines in their oval baking dishes and on the necks of jugs, sometimes using the fingers or, for smaller scale marks, rubber-ended combs.

Thickness gauges

Returning to tools for production rather than decoration, a thickness gauge was often used by throwers, including those at the Dicker Pottery in Sussex and Ewenny Pottery, for checking on the thickness of the base when throwing big wares. It was the shape of a capital 'E', made of wood of about 1 in. square in section, the back of the 'E' being 1 ft long, and the bars half that, the middle one being fixed with a wing-nut through a slot in it. If this adjustment bar is set, say, half an inch shorter than the outer ones, it is easy to see the thickness of the base of the opened-out start of a pot by placing the two outer bar ends on the wheel-head or bat.

Consistency in size was very important when it came to packing the kiln. In order to ensure consistent sizes, some potters, (including some at Buckley), had a set of wooden 'T's, each one cut to a particular standard internal size. It was sufficient to lower the appropriate guide into the first pot of the batch to check both depth and width. When found satisfactory, the guide stick could be set in its lump of clay on the edge of the wheel tray, and no further measurement was necessary. Another way of measuring that first pot was with a notched stick, which could be used even when covered with clay.

CHAPTER FIVE

A. Harris & Sons,
Farnham Potteries, Wrecclesham

AFTER HAVING worked elsewhere nearby, Absalom Harris established the pottery at Wrecclesham near Farnham in Surrey in 1873. He and his team produced a full range of flowerpots and glazed wares (jugs, bread-crocks etc.) as well as extruded bricks, pan tiles and drainage pipes. The Harris family had been potters in the area for some time; I remember seeing a tall chimney pot rouletted 'Harris, Fareham Common'. (Do not be confused between Fareham, on the coast, Farnham near Wrecclesham, and Farnborough, nearer London). By the turn of the 19th century, they were also producing various 'art wares' with a copper-stained galena glaze, to imitate the local Tudor greenwares. After the Second World War, they concentrated on unglazed horticultural wares and decorative flowerpots.

As can be seen from the photographs, in those days they made a wide range of flowerpots, including pedestal pots, wall-pots and rhubarb and seakale forcers. The basis of the production remained however the range of plain flowerpots in a range of sizes, but roughly the same proportions, that is as wide as they were tall. Below is a list of sizes taken from a sgraffito earthenware tile fixed to a beam in what was then Reg Harris' workshop.

(RIGHT) A stack of forcers and their lids, formal garden urns on their pedestals, and stacks of cylinders used inside flowerpots when setting the kiln.

Farnham Potteries, Wrecclesham. All the photographs of the pottery were taken in the late 1970s. The bottle kiln on the left was still in use; the last to be used in England.

No. Size		Height inside	Width inside top
1		18 in.	20¼ in.
2		15¾ in.	18 in.
3		14½ in.	15¾ in.
4		12¼ in.	13½ in.
6		11½ in.	12 in.
8		10¼ in.	10½ in.
12		9½ in.	9¾ in.
16		8¼ in.	8½ in.
24		7¼ in.	7¼ in.
32		6¾ in.	6¾ in.
48		5¾ in.	5¾ in.
60		4 ⅜ in.	4 in.
60	(small)	4 in.	3½ in.
72		3½ in.	3⅛ in.
72	(small)	3	2½ in.
48	(special sm)	5	5
32	(special sm)	6	6

The pottery

When I was a student in the 1970s, I, like many others, used to visit the pottery when I could, to see Reg Harris and his cousin Fred Whitbread, Absalom's descendents, both of whom were remarkably kind and tolerant of visiting students. By that date the pottery building was not in good repair, in fact one wing was already roofless and abandoned. In spite of this, the two potters, usually with one assistant, continued production as they always had.

One entered from the courtyard into a dank drying room, the small windows and slatted floor above giving only limited light on the boards and boards of damp flowerpots. Upright poles, with horizontal 'shot pins' (lengths of hazel rod) supported the wareboards. With the dim light and the smell of old earth, it was like stepping into

Slatted boards of drying pots in the back upstairs workshop.

another world, or another time. Somewhere above, the motor of Reg's wheel rumbled continuously.

Passing further into the building, off to the right was Fred's workshop, very quiet but for the slap of clay onto the wheel-head or the movement of a potboard. Through at the back of the works was the pugmill and soaking pit. The extruder, a converted hop-press, was in a corner covered with an old plastic sack to keep the clay inside from drying. Further on again was the curved wall of the kiln.

Up some narrow wooden steps, the door for packing the kiln was at first floor level. There were a couple of rooms upstairs with wheels by the windows. Sometimes there would be an apprentice working on one of these kickwheels, and pots everywhere, in various stages of drying. Finally one arrived at Reg's workshop: the wheel near the corner, with a window to its right, piles of bats, and

the wedging bench by another window looking out to the courtyard and entrance.

The Wrecclesham method

A heap of clay lay in the yard behind the works, exposed to the weather. When more was required, the apprentice would be sent with barrow and spade to bring in enough to fill the brick-lined pit. Layer by layer it would be sprinkled with sand and watered with hose or watering-can, then left to soak for at least a couple of days.

After soaking in the pit, the clay was pugged and stored in a stack of extruded blocks, each layer separated from the one below with a sprinkling of sand, and kept covered and damp.

When Reg needed more clay, he would set the pugmill going, take a couple of these blocks and

Reg; knocking-up balls of clay ready for throwing.

which were stored in stacks by the wheel. These were recycled lids from grape boxes from a local grocer, they had two cross-pieces holding the planked disc together. Sticking the bat on a disc of clay on the wheel-head with a little slurry, these cross-pieces gave a good 'key' ensuring they would not budge.

Reg Harris throws a large flowerpot

The bat would be dampened with the palm of the hand, the lump of clay put on, and the whole wetted once the wheel got going. First the sides are pushed in and slightly up, ensuring the lump is well fixed. Then with the heel of the right hand the clay is pushed down, at the edge and in the centre, forming a curved dip in the top, which is already the start of opening-up. The middle fingers of the right hand, backed up by those of the left, push down in the middle, right to the bat, forming the central drainage hole. Moving the fingers up the thickness of the base or a little more, they are moved back towards the potter, becoming more clenched as they move back, more or less finishing the base of the pot. By now the wall is a thick conical cylinder which is then compressed, widened a little, and the rim made round and thick. Fingers and knuckle back to the bottom, and the wall is drawn up to half its height in a first lift.

Now the second, this time pushing in dramatically with the edge of the right hand, palm upwards, and the wall is thinned and moved upwards until slightly higher than the guide stick. The lifting done, the rim is again compressed and brought out to its required diameter.

Now taking the square rib from the edge of the wheel-tray by the water bowl, the wall of the pot is brought out to its final profile, first using the rib from the base up to the rim in a couple of moves, pushing out with the inside fingers.

With the pot now nearly completed, it is almost time to pass to the finishing touches, time to form the 'rope' decoration.

Again the rim is trued and consolidated, and with the corner of the rib a line is drawn to show where the prepared coils of clay are to be joined. Drying his hands, first on the edge of the wheel tray, then further by pivoting them flat on the

pass them through the pugmill a second time. Up some stairs to his workshop, and they would be stacked on the bench. Even for larger pots, the amount of clay was judged by the number of grabs of clay.

To make a lump of clay sufficient for a big flowerpot, he would take two grabs of the soft clay with cupped fingers, and slap them together, tear this in half and slap them together again, in a small-scale version of wedging (as described before, with a wire). After a few tears and slaps, the cake of clay, perhaps 3 lbs or so, was put on the bench, and a couple more grabs of clay taken from the block. The process was repeated, and the second cake was slapped onto the first and so on, until the right amount had been built up and the resulting lump of clay swivelled and slapped into a short cylinder. Those in the photographs would weigh about 30 lbs (see p.58–9).

Bigger pots were thrown on the wooden bats

Throwing sequence, showing Reg Harris at the wheel.

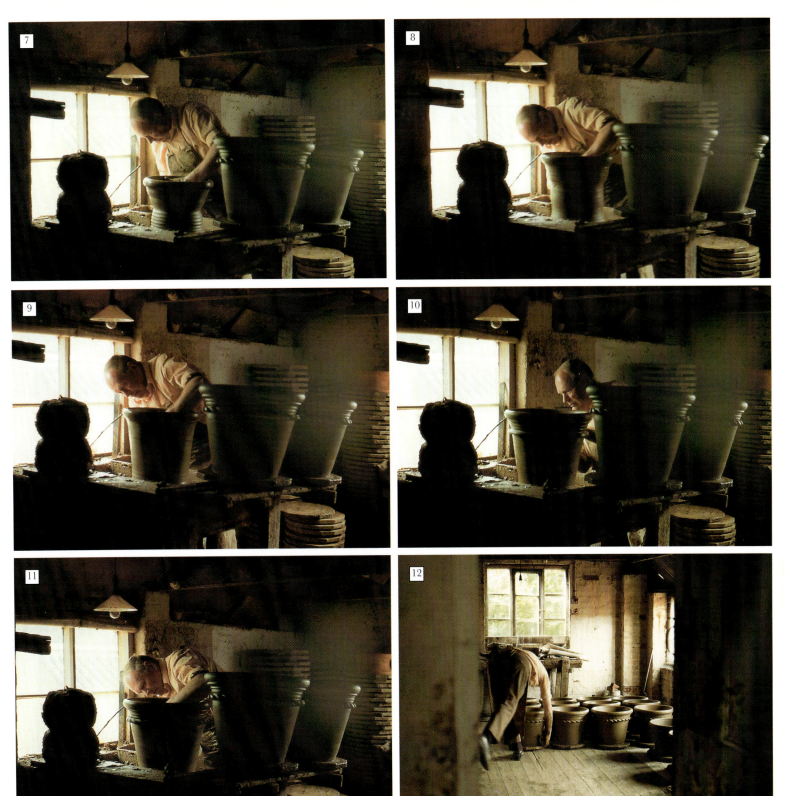

wareboard, he reaches for the bat with the coils from the bench. Wetting the inner side of the coils, they are gently pressed round the line. Three lengths make the tour. With the wheel going again, and the fingers inside supporting, a wet sponge is pressed over the coil, one finger above and one below the coil, so that it is thrown on and triangular in section. Putting the sponge down, and the wheel turning very slowly, the coil is then pushed up with the side of the right forefinger rhythmically as the pot turns, still with the left hand supporting inside.

The decorative rope formed, the rib is again taken up and the wall of the pot is smoothed once again, this time from the coil downwards, the supporting edge of the left forefinger on the interior in the final shaping. Then he would sponge the water from inside the pot, and rib the base of the pot smooth, paying particular attention to the point where the base meets the wall.

At last the wire-cut. With the wheel still going, and the wire held down on the bat, he would cut away from himself until he saw the wire in the central drainage hole. After a couple of turns of the wheel, he would then draw the wire back towards himself. As ever at Wrecclesham, the wareboard of pots on their bats was only removed when the board was full, and the next pot finished on the wheel.

Production always seemed unhurried, but steady, and Reg would use above five tons of clay in a fortnight. It is a measure of this clay's propensity to stand up on the wheel that they could add the coils for rope decoration to the freshly thrown pot; with many clays one would have to wait until the pot was firmer. Flowerpots are traditionally ribbed smooth on the exterior (using the rib tool). This is said to make them more resistant to attack from woodlice and other pests than pots with throwing-rings showing. 'Louse-ladders' Reg used to call them.

Throwing smaller pots

Downstairs in Fred's workshop, in low light, he made all the small flowerpots essential for filling the spaces between the larger ones in the kiln. Working on the smooth running kickwheel, it was always impressive to see this master craftsman, whose lifetime's work had honed his skill to what appeared to be total ease. One process flowed into the next in

a calm rhythm, and soon another board of pots would be finished, then another pot, and he would rise from his seat to move the wareboard across to a rack and get an empty one to replace it at the side of the wheel. After placing the pot from the wheelhead on the farthest corner of the wareboard, it was back to throwing. Like Reg, he would fetch a fresh block of clay from the pugmill, but having got it, he simply put it on its end on the transverse board on his wheel.

Installed on the seat of the wheel, Fred would take a grab of the soft clay from this block, with the cupped fingers of his hand, and throw it onto the centre of the wheel-head where the wire-cut mark of the previous pot remained. With a dip of the right hand to gather some water, the grab of clay was first squeezed in and up, then down into a low perfectly centred cylinder. If, by feel, it was not quite enough clay, another grab was taken, this time with two fingers, and this was slapped onto the middle of the previously centred lump, but he usually got it right first time. With a continuous flow, centring would change to opening. In went the right thumb, right to the wheel-head, making the drainage hole. Moving up, the thumb moved outwards, in one sweep forming the base of the pot. More water, and the wall is thrown up in a slightly conical form and, with the second lift, it becomes almost the finished shape.

At this stage, if a thick rim is required, the rim is splayed out and folded down onto itself before being compressed and smoothed by the skin between the first two fingers. Then with a square rib in the right hand, the left hand fingers push the wall onto the rib from bottom to top giving the final smooth profile. Water sponged out, the wire is passed right through at wheel-head level. The palms of the hands are scraped clean on the edge of the square wheel-tray, and the pot would be touched off-centre with the right hand, and caught with the left, all this with a twisting motion, following the rotation of the wheel. The pot is then placed next to the last on the wareboard. Without hesitation in the next move, the cupped fingers are already taking the next grab and slapping it into the middle of the wheel.

Flowerpots, particularly small sizes, must be very accurately made if they are to 'nest' properly, one in the next, in the tall stacks in which they are

(TOP) Fred Whitbread at his geared kickwheel.

(ABOVE) Fred's small workshop looking towards the opposite end from the wheel.

fired. Not only must the rim be the right diameter and height, as gauged by the stick stuck in a lump of soft clay on the side of the wheel-tray, they must also have a consistent angle of wall, with a small base to fit the interior of the next pot in the stack.

At Wrecclesham, the clay was used very soft, which made centring relatively easy and fast. There were many tiny air bubbles in the clay, which one could hear crackle and pop as the potters threw, as if in the souring of the clay there was some fermentation going on. Whether these miniscule bubbles acted somehow like grog, allowing the clay to stand up, or for some other reason, it was remarkable how soft it could be used, even for throwing big pots.

I must admit that in my description of Fred throwing, I was not quite accurate about lifting-off. He was in the habit of momentarily stopping his wheel to lift off, as they used to do when working with a 'passer' (assistant). It was however normal practice for throwers working on their own to lift off small flowerpots (up to 15cm/6 in. ones) without stopping the wheel. It was in this way they lost no time and were able to throw three pots per minute.

I have a weakness for finding old books in second-hand bookshops. In one such book, I found the following poem. It immediately reminded me of Fred at his kickwheel. It is full of gentle humour and hidden depths!

The Potter*

The potter stood at his daily work,
One patient foot on the ground,
The other with never slack'ning speed,
Turning his swift wheel round.

Silent we stood beside him there,
Watching the restless knee,
Till my friend said low, in a pitying voice,
'How tired his foot must be!'

The potter never paused in his work,
Shaping the wondrous thing;
'Twas only a common flower pot,
But perfect in fashioning.

Slowly he raised his patient eyes,
With homely truth inspired,
'No, Marm; it isn't the foot that works;
The one that stands gets tired.'

Anonymous

*(From 'Tommy's First Speaker' published by M. A. Donohue & Co., Chicago, and reprinted in *Industrial Arts for Elementary Schools*, see bibliography).

(OPPOSITE ABOVE) Sliding the board further along. (OPPOSITE BELOW) Some of Fred's production in the pottery yard. Standard sizes in some potteries went down to these tiny two-inch 'thumb-pots', just big enough to grow one seed.

CHAPTER SIX

Isaac Button

and the

Soil Hill Pottery

MR BUTTON HAS become something of a cult figure over the years. He was brought to the notice of the wider pottery community by the film made about his work by John Anderson and Robert Fournier in 1965, 'Isaac Button, Country Potter'. Although there were other country potters still working,

Button was perhaps the last to be producing such a full range of glazed domestic pots as well as flowerpots. Because of the film however, he was the one who has come to epitomise the romantic image of the lone heroic country potter.

The pottery, sometimes known as the Ogden Potteries, is at Holmfield, between Halifax and

FIG 6 Sketch plan of Soil Hill Pottery, not to scale, roughly as it was in the early 1960s.

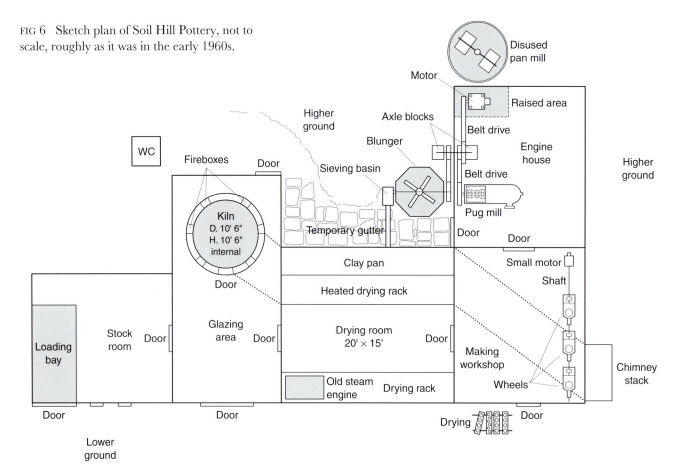

The works, when still in production. *Photograph by R. Fournier.*

Keighley in Yorkshire. It had been started by the famous Jonathan Catherall of Buckley in the late 18th century, and stayed in the possession of the Catherall family until the late 19th century. For a while it was worked by a member of another well-known potting family, John Kitson, but by this time it was pretty run down. Towards the end of the 19th century it was bought by Isaac Button, (confusingly) the grandfather of the one in the film.

This first Isaac seemed to have been something of a pioneer potter; having bought the near-derelict works, he started work at the site by producing hundreds of bricks, which were clamp-fired. He had started out as a brick-maker, before changing careers to become a potter. With these bricks an entirely new pottery works was built further down the hill and the old building demolished.

This new pottery was particulary well planned, and was quite innovative, incorporating steam powered machinery. It introduced to the area the first downdraught kiln, whose flue-ways not only passed under the clay-settling pan, but also under drying racks in the long drying room. The slope of the hill was cleverly used, so that where the clay arrived at the blunger was on higher ground, to be at the right level for loading it. From the bottom of the blunger, there was enough change in level so that sieving could take place, and the short wooden gutter would carry the flow of slip into the drying pan. From here the floor levels were the same throughout, so that at the far end of the building, down the hill, there was enough change in outside ground level to have a sunken loading bay for loading the wares onto wagons, and later lorries. A large door opposite the kiln facilitated coal deliveries.

The long building, with the engine house forming the foot of an 'L', was organised to suit the flow of production. The heavy machinery (the blunger and pugmill) were conveniently near the steam engine (later replaced by an electric motor), and the pugmill conveniently by the door where the clay was barrowed in from the drying pan. Next door was the throwing room, then the 20 ft by 15 ft drying room, the kiln, the ware store and finally the loading bay. Not only did it have the various raw materials on site, but it was near the highly populated mill towns which boomed in the 19th century.

Arthur followed his father (the first Isaac) into the business, as did the next generation, the two brothers (even more confusingly) Arthur and the famous Isaac, although Arthur left the pottery shortly after the Second World War. Before the war there had been a workforce of 13, firing the 500 cu. ft kiln once a week. From 1947 until 1964 Isaac Button continued on his own, apart from having a helper for firings, who took some of the shifts in the 48 hour firing schedule. He fired every six or nine weeks, depending on what kind of wares were in production; it took less time to fill it with bread-crocks than with pancheons for example.

It was not *only* a life of unremitting toil, for Mr Button had a social life, and two boys to bring up on his own after the death of his wife. Perhaps this was what kept him going so long.

Potters Sheila and Robert Fournier became aware of the pottery in the mid-1950s, and became regular visitors, sometimes helping out with jobs like glazing, or joining the parts of puzzle-jugs, a job Mr Button disliked. He preferred doing a run of production rather than 'fussy' jobs. He was always somewhat bemused by their interest in his work, and sometimes confessed he would be just as happy being a car mechanic. Later, in several visits from 1961 to 1964, Robert Fournier and cameraman John Anderson made the film. Their total budget was £200.

The Soil Hill method

With an easy rhythm, the clay was dug at the pit up the hill and shovelled onto the old flat-bed lorry. This relic had tyres filled with clay, and a petrol tank suspended under the driver's seat with a piece of string. Back at the pottery, it was unloaded ready to be gradually shovelled in the blunger. Before a firing, the Boulton blunger was started up, the belt-drive coming from a drive-shaft which extended from a hole through the wall of the engine-house. With the water from a reservoir a little way up the hill, the clay soon broke down to a slip, and the stop cock opened near the base of the tank. This flowed into the sieve which, being suspended by chains,

could be rhythmically bumped against the side to help the slip on its way. Under the sieve was a basin which overflowed into a removable wooden gutter across the paved walkway into the drying pan.

The parallel flues from the kiln passed below the drying pan and the drying racks on their way towards the chimney stack. They were some 4 ft in depth. After a firing, when the water had been evaporated from the clay to the right degree, it was lifted and barrowed into the pottery to be pugged and stored, to sour for a few weeks. Before use, it was put through the pugmill again before being weighed and wedged to make it ready to throw.

Although at least one of the wheels was a 'Boulton' cone-type wheel, Mr Button seems to have made most things on his disc-drive 'Armitage' wheel. It was fitted with a cross-bar to enable him to stand when making taller pots (see p. 4).

The throwing room

The shaft which drove the row of three wheels had a separate motor, after the large motor had been installed to replace the old steam engine. There was also another motor in the throwing room, this was the 7 h.p. motor for a fan which was put in when they reduced the height of the chimney stack by 20 ft, making it only 60 ft tall. It was found that the blast of the icy wind was so great that the top 20 ft had to be regularly replaced, so this was an alternative means of creating a good draught at the beginning of the firing cycle, when the stack was too cold to draw efficiently. It must be said the site is somewhat exposed to the weather; the summit of Soil Hill is 1320 ft above sea-level.

The different pots that were made by Mr Button were made with a variety of hardness of clay. When the film-makers turned up on a day when he was throwing flowerpots with softish clay and asked him to make a big brewing jar, which really required harder clay, he obliged. There was a certain glint in

(OPPOSITE ABOVE) Reversing towards the blunger with a load of clay. On the left the disused pan mill from brick-making days, and right of the lorry the roof over the kiln, with the ladder used to climb up to take test pieces when firing. *Photograph by R. Fournier.*

(BELOW) In the long drying room. *Photograph by J. Anderson.*

(ABOVE) Button pots. In the last few years of his career, Mr. Button could no longer get galena, so changed to using bisilicate frit on the outsides of the pot, and red lead for the interior.

(OPPOSITE) Slipping pancheons, 1961. *Photograph by J. Anderson.*

his eye when he succeeded. Slipping the pots was done when they were hard leather-hard; just starting to show some white on the rim. Glazing was at a similar stage, although some shapes could be glazed when dry (see glazing, p. 81). A standard bread-crock took 24 lbs (11kg) of clay and 70 seconds to throw. Other wares in the range included various sizes of pancheon and flowerpots, including two styles of strawberry pot (one with added half bowls), straight and rounded stew pots, brewing jars, pigeon nests, dog bowls, jugs, mugs

and hen waterers. The biggest thing he made in one piece was a 70 lb brine pot, which seems to have been an earthenware imitation of those often produced by salt-glaze pipeworks; cylindrical in form, with two or four handles added (each the shape of a quarter-sphere in the salt-glazed variety).

Isaac Button retired and sold up in 1964. He moved to Torbay but soon got bored and returned to Yorkshire with the intention of setting up again, in a small way, as a potter. These plans did not progress very far, as he fell ill and died in 1969 at the age of 66.

Isaac Button and further throwing techniques

Academics rightly avoid describing the process of throwing. The techniques take time and practice to learn and, without some familiarity with them, it is hard to judge just how skilful the traditional potters were. One should not be deceived by the seeming ease with which they made apparently simple pots. Whether or not one wishes to emulate it, their ways of working and their skills were of a high order, coming from a flow of tradition that stretched back through centuries.

Having already seen some of the techniques used in throwing flowerpots at Wrecclesham, let us now examine how Isaac Button made a similar pot. As an illustration of the fact that no two potters have the same technique, Mr Button's style was quite different from Reg Harris' but just as effective.

Firstly, everything was thrown directly on the wheelhead. This cuts out having to move pots off bats, and having to clean them. It also means that the slight marks left by lifting off have to be accepted by the customer. Another consequence of lifting off is that the clay must be slightly less soft than that used by Reg Harris.

At the wheel

The clay, which has been weighed, is firmly plunked onto the wheel-head. Centring comes in the usual two moves; first pushing inwards bringing any off-centredness to the top with both hands. Then, still with the left hand on the outside of the cylindrical ball, the right hand pushes down,

Centring completed.

Opening up, and forming the base.

Swelling out with square metal rib.

Forming the rim.

Photographs from J. Anderson.

First pull.

Second pull, thinning the wall.

Ribbed to the final shape, the stew pot rim gets a final shaping.

Adding a handle to the leather-hard stew pot with wetted hand. The piece of clay for the next one awaits on the tressle.

finishing the centring and making a depression in the top of the clay. A hole is formed to the wheel-head, then both thumbs are thrust in, pushing away from the potter and forming the base of the pot. A ring of clay rides on the outer wall. With the right hand inside, thumb over the rim, this is brought out to make a slightly taller shape, the rim being encompassed and compressed by the skin between thumb and fingers. Meanwhile the left hand is still flat on the exterior, as it was for centring. Now that there is more room, the base is smoothed across and compressed. With the hands back to their previous position, the wall is moved up and in to form a cone with a fat rim, the hands still on the left, with the clay coming anti-clockwise toward the potter. The rim is compressed and better defined. With another gather of water, he changes sides; left hand inside, and right on the exterior.

The cone of clay is already half the required height or more. In one lift the pot is thrown up to slightly over the required height, the rim brought out to the correct size and further compressed. Now with his rectangular steel rim, he pushes the bottom in slightly more and, with the left hand on the inside, the wall is trued up to its final profile from the base up to the rim. He sponges out the water, and again the rim gets a little more attention. Reaching for the roulette from the water pot, he brings it to the wall of the pot and pushes it on, supported on the inside by the side of the left index finger. One circuit, not too much overlap, and the pot is wired off. Scraping his hands on the edge of the metal wheel-head, he puts them round the pot, as low as possible, with little fingers resting on the wheel-head so that any compression is supported by the horizontal base. Using a forearm for further contact, he lifts the pot off to the wareboard. The more contact the palms of the hands and forearms have with the pot, the less compression is required; like a ladder on thin ice, the load is spread.

Lifting off: various techniques

For larger pieces, a 'cow's rib' or lifting-off stick is used. This is simply a curved piece of wood, perhaps 1 ft long, and flattish in section. When the pot has been wired through, the stick is placed against the wall of the pot, fairly low down, then

(ABOVE) Mr. Button applies the roulette wheel to the freshly thrown flowerpot before wiring off. *Photograph by J. Anderson.*

(BELOW) Lifting-off a brewing jar using the 'cow's rib'. The hands, fore arms and stick give all-round support. *Photograph by J. Anderson.*

the hands go on, round the far side of the pot, low down so that the stick's ends are lying across the forearms. It is remarkable how little distortion occurs when big pots are lifted off in this way. One can often see the marks left by the hands, forearms and stick on some old country pots.

At Fremington they used a bit of old cheese-ring as a lifting-off stick. Some of the examples on show at Wetheriggs are slightly more sophisticated; broad and flat in the middle, they curve up to narrow ends. These curves fit the convexity of the forearms. They are rather like the slats from local ladder-backed chairs. Another way of lifting off big pots was to do it with an assistant at right angles to the thrower. They both put the palms of the hands on, and lifted together. As one might expect, this was the method employed at Verwood.

Mr Button had another trick for lifting off bottle forms; this was to place a rolled-up ball of clay on the rim, thus sealing in the air. Since the air could not escape, it was like lifting a balloon, reducing the risk of distortion from the hands or cow's rib. With the pot safe on the board, the ball was removed, and saved for the next pot.

Techniques for throwing big and small pots

Another technique that can be seen in the film 'Isaac Button, Country Potter' was specific to big-ware throwing. When making a brewing jar or bread-crock, Mr Button would divide his clay into two parts. First he would centre and flatten a 6 lb lump into a slightly domed disc. Onto this he would throw the main lump of clay, say 22 lb, centre it, and throw the pot. The reason for this was that it was a way to avoid trapping air bubbles under a large lump of clay on the worn wheelhead.

For small pots of 2 lb or so, like the dog bowls shown in the film, Mr Button had what was almost a one-handed method of throwing. Although the left hand is there supporting, all the action is with the right. Having centred the clay, the right thumb goes in and opens out the base, then smoothes it across again. Keeping his thumb on the inside, he uses the fingers to push in and up to make the wall. Another similar lift, and the full height is achieved. The rib is brought in for the final shaping, and after a bit more attention to the rim, which turns in, the pot is wired off and completed.

A variation on this technique was often used for throwing flowerpots in this and other potteries. The clay was centred and opened with both thumbs pushing away from the potter on the far side of the wheel-head. The position of the hands then remained the same and the initial cone pulled up towards the potter, thumbs inside and fingers outside, all on the far side of the pot. This technique was used in Ireland and is beautifully demonstrated by Paddy Murphy in a film made for Irish television written and narrated by the actor Ray McAnally. It was one of a series of craft films entitled 'Hands', and the pottery is still in production at Ennerscorthy, in County Wexford in the south-east of Ireland.

Adapting the wheel

The wheels that potters used generally had the seat level with the surface of the wheel-head. In some of the potteries in the south of England, when making small wares, they would raise the throwing level by 3 or 4 in. so that it was level with the top of the kickwheel's square wheel-tray. This they did by throwing a solid hump of clay the shape of an upturned bowl, and sticking a bat upon it. This bat acted as a raised wheel-head for the day's throwing. By contrast, for big ware production, the seats were raised up, sometimes using a block of wood, and cross-bars were installed so that the potter could get into a higher position over the pot (see photograph on p. 49).

Two-part throwing

The essential quality of country pots, or one of them, is their directness and lack of fuss. Whenever possible they would be made in one piece, and entirely finished on the wheel at the time of throwing. When the pot was taller than the length of the thrower's arm, however, this could not be done; for example, with tall chimney pots, forcing bells for rhubarb, and some of the biggest sizes of crock.

Of course, every potter had his own methods. Some chimney pots were made thus: a first section (or rather, a batch of them) was made like a large flowerpot with no base, and a good round rim, which later would serve to hold the chimney pot in its mortar. Then a batch of second stages were thrown, also with no base, but the right way up, including a robust rim and sometimes a 'rope'

Large crock made in two sections. A larger version of the crock in p. 29. Instead of ham pans, many potteries in the north made large 'flesh pots' for salting meat, often with four handles. This example was photographed at 'Below Stairs' antiques shop, Hungerford, with their kind permission.

Reg Harris used to join the sections of rhubarb forcers using the old hand-cranked wheel. With the clay still relatively mobile, he took the precaution of wrapping a wet string a couple of times round the top of the first section before adding the second.

Sometimes, coils were added to rims of the first sections of pots in the manner of Cretan oil-jars. Once added, the coil is thrown up, but the method is limited in the height that can be gained with each coil. Nethertheless, this is the preferred method used today by Mick Pinner and Svend Bayer (see Chapter 12) for the production of chimney pots and very large flowerpots.

Another method widely used for both chimney pots and forcers is still practised by Peter Strong at Wetheriggs (see Chapter 12). A large lump of clay is thrown on a bat to make a tall flowerpot shape, leaving a large hole in the base, and a good thickness of clay. This base is kept damp (nowadays with plastic) for a couple of days until the rim is hard enough to support the weight of the pot. A large bat is placed on the rim, and the whole thing turned over, preferably by two people. The first bat can be wired off and removed, and the pot on its new bat centred up on the wheel. The thick section is thrown upwards and inwards to continue the line of the pot and, in the case of rhubarb forcers, a rim to take a lid is made. The advantage of the technique is that a smooth continuous profile can be achieved as there is no join.

decorative band below it, both sections having been thrown on bats. After a day or two, the first sections could be turned over onto another bat and cut off the first. The first stage, now upside down, could be moved back to the wheel-head and moved to the centre. After some 'keying' with an old fork, and wetting with slurry, the second stage would be put on top and the join consolidated and smoothed with a rib on the outside and the left hand inside. Since the two sections were joined at their softest part, that is, where they had been joined to the bat, the potter could move the stiffened clay enough to get the profile right. Sometimes, particularly for very tall multiple-section chimney pots, it was not convenient to move them back to the wheel, and the sections were simply 'luted' together and the join scraped and smoothed as well as possible. Inevitably this gave a slightly more uneven profile.

Handles

VERTICAL HANDLES

As with throwing, each potter made handles in their own way. In Fremington, to make a jug handle, they pre-pulled them, a little thicker than required, from a long 'carrot' of clay and laid them in a row along the bench. They were nipped from the length by the thumb in such a way as to give a curved end suitable for pushing onto the rim of the jug. Once on, it was only a matter of two or three pulls to give it the required section and the bottom could be joined, nipped off, and smoothed on. In this way they could do the job remarkably quickly; a hundred or more per hour.

At Brannams, a standard day's throwing would produce 300 medium-sized jugs. Handling,

Large water jug from South Wales, ht. 18 in. (approx.), possibly from the Bargoed Pottery near Cardiff. Cornish pitcher typical of Lakes of Truro (see p. 31) with its robust handle and thin coating of white slip. A little brown jug again from south Wales, the glaze a reddish brown. Apart from Ewenny and the above, there were other potteries in south Wales, e.g. Nantgawr. Finally, a small Fremington milk jug, ht. (5½ in.).

Buckley 'mutton' pressed dish, 12.5in x 10 in.
Pot from the Bell-Hughes collection.

decorated later, once it had been taken off the mould. This sequence of different techniques is a demonstration of the fall from prestige that such wares suffered over the years, so that faster more direct methods were employed. The Buckley dishes with this raised trailing include the ones with the words 'beef', 'mutton', 'duck' etc. written across the base.

All the above dishes were made on hump or 'drape' moulds made of biscuit clay, or more usually wood. Since the wall of the dish is of even thickness throughout, and they are formed soft, they do not have stresses caused by the throwing process, and are therefore resistant to thermal shock.

Similar rectangular dishes were made in the north-east of England in great quantities, often with their distinctive dividers across the middle. By contrast with the Buckley ones, these were made in concave moulds, probably made of plaster. This can be seen from their precise outer shape, and the slight scars on the exterior of the walls, where the slab has been laid on the mould prior to being pressed down into it. The edge of the mould leaves its mark on the soft clay. Adding a divider made with an off-cut from the dish slab can thus be done immediately the dish has been formed. It can be well pressed home, as the dish is supported by the mould. The dish can be turned out of the mould immediately, as the long walls, which might otherwise have a tendency to sag, are held in by the dividing wall. Was the divider a clever device for fast production, or to divide sweet and savoury

(TOP) Big dishes from the north-east of England, 17½ in. x 14 in.

(ABOVE) More variations on the theme. *Morton collection.*

foods, or just to hold the pastry up? Perhaps all of these things. These dishes came in a great range of sizes. Some are as big as a kitchen sink (a shallow one) and there is quite a variation in their shapes. They have the advantage of being an item that even a beginner in the pottery could produce with little training or experience.

Extrusion

At Wrecclesham, like many other flowerpot works, they used an extruder to produce square and rectangular seed pans, window box pots, as well as the long bricks used in packing the bottle kiln. A block of clay from the pugmill was put into the box of the extruder. By means of a lever and ratchet system, the clay was pushed horizontally towards and through a die plate at the end, by means of a steel plunger. Extruded walls were cut and rejoined to form the ends of the pot. Rectangular shapes are particularly favoured by horticulturalists, since by using them they lose less bench-space in the greenhouse.

At Fremington there was a big vertical extruder, with a large and heavy flywheel which drove a screw-thread. At the end of this shaft was a plate, the 'driver', which was thus pushed down the cylindrical barrel towards the die plate. They made various sizes of pan rings with die plates with a thick 'L' cut in them. Agricultural land-drainage pipes were made with die plates whose central disc was supported by bridge-pieces behind the die. Whatever the details of this machine, it must have been effective, since land drains were a major part of the output of the pottery.

Bread ovens

A speciality of Devon and Cornish potteries, these 'Cornish ovens' were also known as 'cloam ovens'. Cloam is a dialect word meaning earthenware. They were used throughout the two counties, as well as being shipped to south Wales, and earlier in the 17th century also to North America. They were made up until about 1930. When Brannams of Barnstable bought the old Fremington Pottery shortly after the First World War, they kept on Bill

(TOP) The extruder at Wrecclesham; cutting table on the left, the box of the extruder covered with plastic, and the long handle leaning against the wall.

(ABOVE) Freshly made seed pans and other extruded wares in the gloom of the downstairs drying room where one entered the pottery. All this work made by Fred Whitbread.

Short from the old Fremington staff, and he continued making saggars and ovens at the old works throughout the 1920s.

Fishley-Holland learned how to make these ovens as part of his apprenticeship training at Fremington. Coarse rounded grit from the River Torridge was used to 'temper' the clay. They had a set of iron frames of different sizes for the different standard sizes of oven. They were horseshoe shaped, with a straight side where the gap in the horseshoe would be. The appropriate size would be

FIG 7
Bread oven.

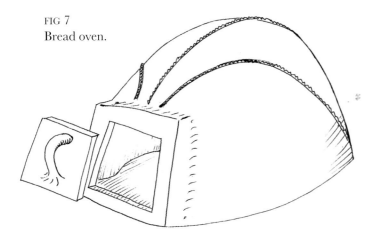

placed on the wooden floor, and sand sprinkled liberally within it. The rough clay would be put in, and trodden out flat to fill the frame. On a board, a slab for the back was similarly trodden out. This board, its centre moved round to the back of the curve of the horseshoe base, was carefully put on edge, and the two ends of the slab curved round and joined, the base having been daubed with slurry in advance. The two ends were temporarily supported by a board until another slab was made for the front and joined, sloping slightly inwards. Now the wall is all the way round it can support itself. By curving it in, the gap is further closed-in, and the front made square. With a little coiling, the dome is completed, and a hole is spiked in the front to let air escape as the oven stiffens.

When soft leather-hard, a door was cut in the front with a knife, and the coiled section smoothed inside. The slab door had a pulled handle added, and coils were added and thumbed to decorate the dome; the pottery stamp was applied above the door, where it would be seen when the oven was installed. There were often other marks or stamps, to ensure the oven had the corresponding door. This completed, the door was put in place for the initial stages of drying. Drying took quite a time; once they had hardened a little, the doors were removed, and the ovens put on end, mouth up to let the air get to the underside. Since the rough sandy clay stood up fairly readily, a whole batch could be made in a day and, in a long day's making, the worker could earn twice his usual pay for making pots.

The ovens were set in the back of the domestic fireplace, and surrounded by at least 1 ft of a good insulating layer: clay, horse dung and chopped straw. Historically they were also used without being built-in. Baking in them was much like in a brick oven; firing them up with a twig fire, pulling the embers, and baking in the falling heat. These cloam ovens were made in a range of sizes, from 2 peck to 12 peck (a peck is 2 gallons or 8 quarts). There is a picture in Artigas' book of women still making similar ovens in Pereruela, north-west Spain in 1968 (see bibliography). There are a few oven makers in Spain to this day.

CHAPTER EIGHT

Glazing and Drying

THE TRADITIONAL GLAZES used for earthenware, whether industrial or hand-made, were all based on oxides of lead. The glazes used tended to be clear, or if there was iron oxide present in the mix, more or less yellow, so the main determining factor for the colour of the pot was the colour of the body or slip below. Over red clay, the clear shiny glaze gives a range of reds, oranges and browns. Over white clay: white, off whites, through a range of yellows. White clays were usually available for slips, and sometimes bodies; red clays were ubiquitous and, to extend the colour range into dark browns to blacks, manganese was commonly and cheaply available to use in slips or occasionally in the glaze. A little copper was sometimes used at Donyatt to imitate earlier more impure glazes, but in the main it was clay, and black or white slip that gave the colours.

The slip, clay reduced to a creamy consistency, was used to give a different colour, usually under the clear glaze. Occasionally it was used on unglazed surfaces, e.g. to give a lighter colour to the pitchers made at Lakes Pottery at Truro (see photograph on p. 75). With the same clear glaze, several colours could be produced, to give a light coloured interior in a pancheon, or for contrasting stripes to an otherwise brownish pot (see photograph on p. 83). A dark coloured slip could equally be used over a light body for the opposite effect (see photographs on p. 13 and p. 82). This allowed most potteries to use just one clear glaze, but if there was demand for a lot of black pots, for example, they could cut out the slipping process and stain the glaze with manganese (see photograph on p. 76).

Dorothey Hartley accurately described the colour of the Buckley pots as being like wallflowers. Since the temperature inevitably varied throughout the kiln, the clay would range in colour from pink through deepening reds until nearly purple when high fired. This gave a range of colours on the glazed surfaces from startling orange to dark browns. For the slip-banded pots the glaze is quite yellow, so probably it had more of the red body clay in the recipe, but for pancheons with white slipped interiors, the glaze was probably made using the same white clay, giving a lighter primrose tone.

It is inevitable that earthenware pots will leak slightly. Crazing or the slightest of pinholes in the glaze are enough to allow the porous body to absorb water. With use this tendency diminishes, as the pores are blocked by oils and baking. The dishes from Buckley were marked for a reason; flavours tend to linger, and one would not bake a rice pudding in a dish marked 'steak and onion'.

Galena and other lead glazes

The Buckley potters got their galena from the nearby leadworks at Halkyn, Rhosesmor, or from Llynpandy. Arriving at the potteries as ore, it had to be ground finely. Here again there was a horse-drawn contraption, the horse plodding its circular path. This time, in the centre, a pair of upright stone wheels rolled round in a circular trough. Later, some had belt driven glaze-mills; after steam, they were driven by a diesel engine. The ore was ground wet, and they also used the same mill to prepare the white slip. At Fremington their glaze-mill seems to have been of a different design, with a

Buckley wash pan, dip pot and lidded milk jug.
From the Bell-Hughes collection.

Buckley dishes.

pair of horizontal stones like a flour mill.

The standard proportions to make a galena glaze (for application by dipping or pouring) are two parts of galena to one part clay (by weight). A white firing clay (not too refractory) gives a clear glaze, while the addition of 3 to 5% of iron oxide, or by using some red body clay in the mixture, will give rich amber tones. The addition of 5% of manganese dioxide makes black, but if too much is

(OPPOSITE PAGE) Buckley Blackware brewing jar. In contrast to the example on p. 76 which seems to have a black glaze. By the evidence of drips of slip on the unglazed part and orange shining through the glaze where the slip is thin, it seems to have the same glaze as the pieces above.
From the Bell-Hughes collection.

added, the glaze becomes metallic-looking. Some potters add a little silica to make a harder, less crazed surface; a typical recipe as used by Isaac Button was 10 parts lead, 5 parts white clay, 1 part flint. Sieving with a 60 mesh sieve is fine enough for a smooth melt.

There is no glaze so sparklingly bright as galena, but as a material, it does have its problems. It tends to flow in the kiln, and for this reason dishes and bowls were only glazed internally, while jugs and bread-crocks are often only partially glazed on the exterior, leaving a good 'margin of error' in case of drips. If fully glazed, they would have to be fired on stilts or other supports, which would only be worth doing for relatively expensive decorative wares.

Mr. Button glazing pancheons with kiln in the background. *Photograph by R. Fournier.*

Because galena (a naturally occuring ore) is lead sulphide (PbS) it has a sulphur content which has to be burnt off in the form of gases. This means there must be a free circulation of air in the kiln; the wares have to be stacked in the kiln in such a way that they are entirely exposed to the kiln atmosphere. There are often blushes of deeper red or even a slight sheen on unglazed surfaces where they were fired in proximity to glazed pots. Bread-crocks and stew pots have to be fired separately from their lids.

Red lead oxide

Mr Button got round this problem by using a glaze with red lead oxide on the interior, and then he could wad the lids as if for salt-glazing and fire the pots with their lids. At Wetheriggs (and other northern potteries) they obtained red lead from Newcastle. As they were firing with coal, and this too can have a sulphur content; (the grade of coal was judged by sulphur content) they found it

preferable to use the red lead. Galena, however, was the preferred source of lead in most country potteries.

Yellow lead oxide

Before the First World War, in southern English potteries, it was common to prepare their own litharge (yellow lead oxide). At Wrecclesham they had a special fireplace where lead (usually scrap) was heated in an iron pot, with a chimney to carry away fumes. At Verwood this was built into the kiln structure, being the only brick-structure around; it also kept the processing of the lead away from the main cob-built workshop. William Smith got his supply in London, in 'pigs' (small bars) of 2½ cwt (250 lbs); two tons made up a wagon-load for the return trip after having delivered pots to town. In his book 'William Smith, Potter and Farmer 1790–1858', Bourne describes its preparation, 'the most injurious part of all the work'. After the lead had become liquid in the pot, it was stirred with a rake-like tool suspended from a chain. 'Then the

Dipping the exteriors of bread-crocks in galena glaze, on the left the brilliant red of the red lead glaze for the inside of pots. The pots in the foreground which are about to be glazed are all bone dry. *Photograph by R. Fournier.*

raking had still to go on as the lead cooled, to bring it to a fine powder' (don't try this at home!).

Applying the glaze

Once prepared, the oxide could simply be brushed onto the pots with a soft 'glazemop' brush, sometimes with the addition of some flour to make it stick better, and applied when the pots were dry. Later, when ready-ground galena became available to the potters of the Crossroads Pottery at Verwood, they continued to apply it in the same way, straight from the packet, with the addition of water and no added clay.

Lead is poisonous and perhaps at its most dangerous in its powdered form. This was a particular hazard in earlier days, when powdered lead was dusted directly onto the pots using a coarse cloth. Galena when dry is a sparkling heavy powder which tends to fall to the floor rather than creating dust. When regulations came in after the First World War

concerning the use of raw lead compounds, they did not include galena because of its negligible solubility.

Unlike galena, red lead oxide, white lead oxide, and litharge (yellow lead oxide) are light powders which make dust in the air which can be breathed in easily. Fishley-Holland described how at Fremington in the 19th century, men got 'belly ache' when crushing the dry red lead using the 'iron trough and pounders'. They later ground galena wet in the glaze-mill, and avoided such problems. As the majority of country potters used galena in wet form, from the grinding to the application by pouring, dipping or brushing, they seldom seem to have suffered lead poisoning.

Potters now tend to use 'fritted' forms of lead, or avoid the danger of lead poisoning by making stoneware, since they are no longer dependent on having to use clay found on site.

At Fremington, the clay they used for the glaze came from Weare Gifford, and was yellow in colour. Fishley-Holland described glazing leather-hard pots with the galena glaze. 'A dipper of glaze

Interior of Lambs Pottery, Buckley, 1909, with pancheons and flowerpots drying rim to rim. *From the D & M Frith collection.*

was put in (a pancheon) and they were whirled in the arms until the glaze covered the pan . . . We tested the glaze for thickness by touching it with a finger and noting the size of the blob that was left. Pitchers would be whirled and inverted at the same time. The glaze came out fanwise when you knew how to do the trick.'

Drying

When the pots are just made, the clay is soft and malleable and cannot easily be handled without distortion and marking the surface. They are left on their wareboards until leather-hard, that is, still mobile, but firm. It is at this stage that handles can be added. As the water in the clay evaporates, the pot shrinks, so that handles joined to a pot which was too dry would crack off because they would shrink more than the pot. Equally, slip must be applied while the pot is still damp, so that all can shrink together with no cracking. Sometimes glaze is also applied at the drying stage, a little harder than leather-hard, since it too has a good proportion of clay in it. It is easier to handle the pots when dry, so most potters preferred to glaze them when dry. A minimal amount of water was absorbed by clays with not much sand in them, so the pots could be packed in the kiln almost immediately. In order to avoid steam causing explosions in the thick pots, they had to be bone dry before being packed in the kiln. A long warm-up and gentle firing cycle ensured any residual moisture would cause no problems.

At Poling Pottery, Mr. Hunt wheels a barrow of fired pots from the kiln through the drying room. When the flowerpots are dry on the boards, they are stacked in dozens on the floor to take up less space. *From the Rural History Centre, University of Reading.*

In the damp climate of Britain, getting large amounts of thick pots dry before firing was never easy; they usually had to do more than just wait. At Farnborough, Bourne describes drying-sheds where raw pots, not yet glazed, were stacked round the walls to about waist height, and turf fires, sometimes augmented by some split oak logs, were made on the floor. With no chimney, smoke filled the rooms and billowed from the sheds, to the occasional annoyance of his neighbours.

Similarly, at Fremington, the drying chambers, full of boards of pots on pole-and-pin racking, had smouldering fires of furze (gorse) on the floor. To keep the frost off on winter nights, 'devils' were made; small coals mixed with soft clay were formed into balls, and burnt under a piece of corrugated iron. These smouldered away, and filled the room with sulphurous smoke, preventing the cold air coming in. Any potter who has seen their pots spirally shredded by frost can appreciate the benefits of the system, in spite of its obvious drawbacks. At the Crossroads Pottery, the pots were put on racks upstairs from the workshop. The scent of the turf fires which burned overnight on the floor and the smoke blackened walls are still there as witness.

Many potteries had more sophisticated systems of drying, with hypocausts running below the racks. At Littlethorpe, the whole of the middle of the long throwing workshop is filled by a racking system over a brick-built horizontal flue-way, while the wheels and benches are on the periphery, well-lit by external windows. The heat and smoke of a small fireplace at one end travels along the

The team at Verwood drying flowerpots and pans outside the workshop in the 1930s.

workshop and back to escape by a vertical chimney. They had such a system in both Ewenny Pottery and Winchcombe. At Wetheriggs, one stretches the length of the old workshop, with large slabs of stone over it, some 60 ft long from fire to chimney. Three feet of horizontal flue to 1 ft of chimney was the standard proportion for such a system, and they must be very well built. Inevitably the slow fire builds up tar, as the smoke slows and cools on its journey. After developing stalactites of tar, one day a spark ignites the whole lot, and a cleansing chimney fire burns its way through. This problem was overcome in the cleverly designed Soil Hill Pottery, where the parallel flues of the kiln pass under the drying rack as well as under the clay-pan. The kiln exhaust is of course far too hot to form tar, but the drying system works best if the kiln is being fired once a week. It was for this reason that, after the Second World War, the old steam engine was moved into the drying room, where it provided both drying heat, and a supply of hot water.

Like any pottery, when the sun shone pots were brought out to be put on either temporary trestles or more permanent racks. For big pots, however, slower drying was required away from direct sunshine. At both Verwood and Wrecclesham the first floor was partially slatted to allow a free circulation of air. Instead of solid floorboards, narrower boards were set with gaps between; similarly at Wrecclesham wareboards which were slatted were used for the later stages of drying large pots.

It was the routine at both Donyatt and Wetheriggs to move all the finished pots to the rooms which also housed the kilns, to take advantage of the warm kilns as they cooled for three days. Not only did they dry well, they were also in the right place for repacking the kiln once it had been emptied.

(OPPOSITE PAGE) Early 1980s, looking down the hypocaust system in the workshop at Littlethorpe. George Curtis at a bench in the distance.

CHAPTER NINE

Kilns and Firing

I N THE ERA OF the country potters, kiln design developed from the most basic style of updraught, into increasingly sophisticated 'bottle' kilns, and ended up with the downdraught kiln with separate chimney stacks.

Hot air tends to rise; the updraught kiln made use of this and had the fire below the chamber where the pots were stacked. The pots at the bottom, near to where the flames entered, tended to get the hottest, so the potters added a chimney to draw the heat further up the chamber and distribute the heat more evenly. This chimney, extending from the cylindrical chamber, gave the distinctive shape of the bottle kiln. The idea of drawing the heat through the chamber, to make it as even in temperature as possible, was further extended in the downdraught kiln. With fireboxes around the outside of the chamber and flue-exit holes in the floor, theoretically the heat is used twice, once as the flames rise in the chamber, and also as the heat is drawn down by the independent chimney stack.

Of course, this does not mean potters on most sites were continually upgrading their technology, far from it. If they had a system that worked they tended to stick with it, and some of the most primitive ones lasted the longest, as in the cases of Verwood and Wrecclesham.

But all these kilns had certain similarities. They were all round in plan, and had a domed chamber (in some cases a temporary dome) which was about as high as it was wide.

The only exception to this commonality is the Newcastle-style kiln built at Littlethorpe in the 1950s. Normally used for brick and tile production, this design has a long rectangular downdraught chamber with coal fireboxes along the two long sides. The flue exits are slots in the floor which lead to a chimney stack at the opposite end from the 'wicket', on the two narrow ends of the rectangle. When it became uneconomic to fire with coal in the 1960s, a smaller electric kiln was installed.

The cylindrical updraught kiln

Returning to round kilns, the most basic form of updraught kiln, cylindric in form, has been used for centuries. With no means of supporting an arch this simple design was still widely used in the first half of the 19th century. Archeologists tend to find floors of demolished kilns, and usually imagine domed structures above, but in most cases the chains of metal banding required for supporting such structures were unavailable to the potters.

The kilns in the Verwood area had a cylindrical chamber 8 to 10 ft (2.5–3 m) in diameter, and were as tall as they were broad. Brick arches over the single firebox supported the floor and extended in transverse walls across the chamber, forming both flue-ways to distribute the flame and heat, and as supports for the wares. The firebox went from front to back of the chamber, under these arches, and extended through the mound of earth and shards which provided support and insulation from the chamber wall to the firemouth, usually within the shelter of a stoking shed. From the photographs of the Crossroads pottery, one can see that the top section of the chamber was extended above the mound. They must have

FIG 9

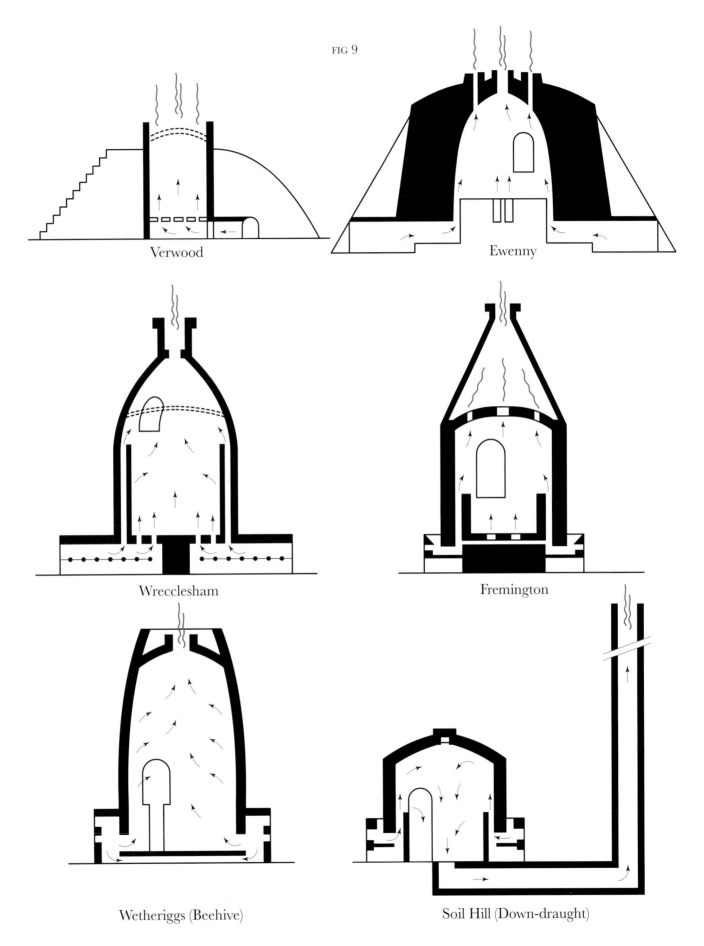

Verwood

Ewenny

Wrecclesham

Fremington

Wetheriggs (Beehive)

Soil Hill (Down-draught)

Drawing the Crossroads kiln in 1928. Mesheck Sims in the kiln passes wares to Jimmy Scammel. Herbert Bailey with the moustache on the left, and Len Sims on the right. Behind the kiln George 'Drummer' Brewer.
Photograph from The Verwood Historical Society.

carefully stacked the bricks for the wicket out of sight for the photography session. This kiln was entirely wood fired, finishing off with furze. Wooden boards, and later sheets of corrugated iron, served as a temporary roof for the kiln between firings, or 'burnings' as they were known there. In its archives, The Verwood Historical Society has a postcard which reads something like 'I shall be returning home because Father's burning'.

A similar kiln is shown in the 1893 photograph at Ewenny (see p. 93). William Smith's kiln at Farnborough was also of this type. Here, as in Verwood, fuel was gathered from the neighbouring common land, heaths where turfs of peat could be dug. Smith got his from Frimley Common as well as the furze (gorse) for the 'bavins' or 'faggots', i.e. the bundles of twiggy material needed for the instant combustion and long flame needed to 'flash' or finish off the firings. These bavins were also used by bakers and most households for firing their bread ovens.

Apart from gorse and hedge cuttings, the 'lop and top' twigs and small branches were bundled up when trees were cut for timber.

A feature of these simple kilns was their lack of firebars; they would only be in the way when firing with bavins.

The Ewenny kiln

The Ewenny Pottery kiln, which had two opposing fireboxes, was later converted into a domed structure. This has been reconstructed at the Museum of Welsh Life at St Fagans. The potters overcame the problem of supporting the domed roof by making the whole chamber a catenary arch, and surrounding it with a thick layer of stonework further supported by heavy butresses. The floor arrangement was also improved. The two fireboxes feed into flues below floor level, round the edge of the circular chamber, and thence into a transversal flue-way across the middle. This latter is separated from the mirror-image flue coming from the other side by a dividing wall, in an attempt to avoid a cross-draught from one firebox to the other, always a problem with such designs. From these

(ABOVE) The same team bringing wares down from the mound at Verwood. One can see from the height of the mound that two-thirds of the chamber is enclosed by it. *Photograph from The Verwood Historical Society.*

(BELOW) The kiln at Ewenny under its temporary roof of boards. Edwin, William and David Jenkins, with oval ham pan in the foreground , and a large water jug similar to that in p. 75. *Photograph from the National Museum of Wales.*

flues, the heat entered the chamber by a series of fireholes round the edge and in the middle. As well as the central exit flue in the dome, there were also four other flue exits. Glaze tests could be drawn from these and, if in one side of the kiln the glaze was maturing earlier than the other side, these flues could be blocked off to divert the flame path to the less melted side. This kiln, about 300 cu. ft, seems to have been fired with coal, and finished off with bavins. It, like all but one of the kilns at Brannams of Barnstaple, north Devon, had no metal grates in the fireboxes. Loose firebricks were gradually built up during the early stages of the firing to the 'glut' arch, the brickwork arch at the top of the entrance to the ashpit. Then, in the more sophisticated Brannams kilns, stoking continued from the smaller firedoors above, while the open brickwork allowed air to pass through the embers.

Beehive kilns

At Littlethorpe and at Wetheriggs they had 'beehive' kilns, and the latter example still stands. Again, there is no extended chimney to form a bottle shape; the chamber is a slightly conical cylinder, but now there are plenty of metal bands, like those round a barrel, holding the whole structure together. The flue exit is simply a round hole in the centre of the dome. Round the base of the kiln, eight coal fireboxes would feed heat into the chamber. Part of this heat flowed up the triangular spaces formed between the square shelves. These shelves were set with upright slabs of fireclay to form 'cupboards'. The rest of the heat from the fireboxes was drawn across radial flues to emerge through a central firehole. Unusually for an updraught kiln, the chamber tended to fire hotter at the top, up to 1120°C (2048°F), than at the bottom, around 950°C (1742°F). With the chamber 10 ft in diameter packed 12 ft high, a yield of 6000 pots could be obtained from a 36 hour firing cycle, using six tons of coal. In spite of all the brickwork and heavy furniture, these gentle giants of kilns did allow economies of scale; the long firings ensured that the sulphur burnt off, and the density of packing ensured fairly even temperatures throughout. As at Soil Hill, the potters at Littlethorpe and Wetheriggs used the best grades of coal with the lowest sulphur content. With the crocks, stew pots, jugs and salt kits in the fixed cupboards, the central area was set with bungs of pancheons, flowerpots, and sometimes saggars.

Bottle kilns

Bottle kilns, like the one at Wrecclesham, also relied on heavy metal banding. They incorporated a conical chimney, which meant that they could be built within a building, so setting could be done from a first-floor level door, and the heat of the kiln could help drying. The Wrecclesham kiln had four fireboxes fired until the mid-1960s with coal, finishing off with bavins, after that it was converted to fire with oil-burners, one in each firebox.

The bottle kiln at Lakes of Truro had a partial dome at the top of the chamber, with a wide circular flue exit in the centre. After packing the bottom of the chamber through a 'wicket' in the chamber wall, this was sealed up, and the setting completed from this annular balcony in the conical part of the kiln. This kiln had four fireboxes for coal and furze, as did those at Winchcombe and Fremington, but in these two at the top of the chamber there was a complete dome, pierced by a

Packing the kiln at the Lakes of Truro; taken from the 'balcony' or partial dome. *From the R. Lloyd collection.*

central round flue exit, as well as other peripheral flues as described on the Ewenny kiln. The conical second chamber thus formed was occasionally used for low-fired ware, but was usually left empty.

The firing cycle

At Fremington, they could buy furze faggots for half a crown (2 shillings and 6 pence) per 100 delivered. They arrived in the green state and were built up into thatched ricks, like haystacks, to dry out. A hundred was enough for one firing; 25 per fire 'hole'.

Their firing routine in the bottle kiln was typical. Once packed and ready, the kiln was preheated with small fires for a day. That evening, small coals were put on the fires, and covered with cinders and some ash to burn slowly overnight. At 6.30 next morning, firing would start, stoking the four coal fires once every hour. As the temperature in the chamber rose, so the shovelling of coal became more frequent, and in smaller amounts. The firing continued day and night, the potters taking shifts; they knew it would take roughly 36 hours, and would all be over by 12.30 or 3.30 p.m. the second day.

When there was a good red showing, it was time to 'flash' the glaze with the furze. (Flashing here is the process of firing with furze. Flame marks on the exterior of pots is also known as flashing, a

The kilns at Fareham. The one on the left is being fired, the date; 22nd August 1966. Against the shed, stacks of small fired flowerpots. *Photograph by J. Anderson.*

related but different meaning.) They lifted the hot firebars from the fireholes with a shovel, as by now the fires had been moved up onto the grates for some time. The faggots of furze were untied one by one, and a couple of branches at a time were stoked in with long handled 'pikes', a sort of blunt-ended pitchfork. With one man at each firehole, the faggots were stoked onto the already established ember bed. With much crackling and sparks, the furze blazed up, sending long flames through the setting. After about 45 minutes, the embers had built up so much that there had to be a pause; while one man raked back the embers, two others shovelled the excess into a metal pan. The fourth damped the embers down from bread ovens set round the kiln mouth-up and filled with water for this purpose. While two recommenced the stoking, the other two took the pan of embers to the drying chambers, where it was tipped on the floor in a heap. Then it was back to stoking the furze until the next raking-out (describing a firing at Truro, Cardew noted that of a 24-hour firing, the last eight hours of it were fired with furze). When the time came, test pieces were drawn from the kiln with a metal rod. If one side was hotter than the other, stokers would take a rest on the hot side,

while stoking continued on the cool side, until an even melt throughout was achieved. With the fireholes blocked up and clammed, it took the kiln three days to cool. It was a day's work for three men to unpack all the ware, sort it and move it all into the stockrooms.

At Farnborough the whole firing cycle took a week: three days setting, three days firing, and one for unpacking or 'drawing' the kiln, after several days cooling. There was one firing per fortnight.

After a long warm-up with peat, to 200 or 300°C (392–572°F) wood would be used for the main firing until a good red heat was perceived. Then it was time to change to firing with bavins, and the long flames would roar through the shard-covered top of the kiln, until even the outer shards would glow red. In order to gauge when the kiln was hot enough, the potters would observe the colour, but also they would watch the level of the setting. At about 1000°C (1832°C) the clay shrinks, and when the potters packed the kiln they would align the setting with a protruding course of bricks in the kiln wall known as the 'gauge'. When the level of the setting had fallen to say, a brick's width, they knew by experience that the necessary temperature had been attained. Reg Harris

continued to use this method of judging the maturity of the firing when using the bottle kiln at Wrecclesham. The other way the potters could judge when the firing was done, was to withdraw glazed test pieces through a removable brick or 'bung' in the wall of the kiln, or the wicket. When all these signs looked right, the firemouth was sealed to prevent the circulation of air during cooling.

(ABOVE) In the yard at Verwood. Although the Thornes, the owners of the pottery, had a wood business as well, it looks likely that the wood shown here was kiln fuel. The upright entire young pine-trees might be forest thinnings, leaning against the main woodstack. The taller stack of twiggier material on the right is probably the 'bavins', again somewhat hidden by the upright timber and bundles. *Photograph from The Verwood Historical Society.*

(RIGHT) Exterior of the stoking shed shown in p. 104. The cob building abuts the kiln and its mound, and is wide enough to be stacked with wood on either side of the stoking area. Cream pans and some flat dishes dry on their boards on the left. As well as the firemouth, this building also had a smaller fireplace where the lead was prepared (see p. 84). *Photograph from The Verwood and District Potteries Trust Archive.*

The downdraught kiln

The potters were always watching what was going on in the wider industry, and would introduce new equipment if they thought it affordable and appropriate. From the end of the 19th century some potters started using downdraught kilns with a cylindrical chamber and separate chimney stack. Although more expensive to build, with their long flues and chimney stacks, they were slightly more efficient and

even in heat distribution, although when firing to 1000°C (1832°C) the difference was marginal.

Many potteries continued to have new updraught bottle kilns built. Firing a downdraught kiln was not a great change from firing updraught kilns; the fireboxes and domed chamber remained the same. At one stage Brannams had existing updraught bottle kilns converted to downdraught; it was simply a case of building under-floor flue-ways and linking them with a common chimney stack.

As we have seen from the example of Soil Hill near Halifax, there were other benefits to this style of kiln. The Soil Hill kiln, with a chamber of 500 cu. ft had six firemouths, and in the 48 hour firing cycle, 2½ tons of coal were used. The chamber measured 10 ft 6 in. high and 10 ft 6 in. in diameter. In 1925, the Aldridges had a similarly sized one built at Donyatt. It was fired once a week; setting the kiln was on Tuesday and Wednesday, warm-up on Thursday, and that evening the coal fires were banked-up overnight. Firing was on Friday through the night, and by noon on Saturday, it would be ready for 'flashing' with the faggots (bavins). Test pieces were drawn, and Holdcraft bars observed (these bars are similar to pyrometric cones, they sag into ceramic cradles when predetermined amounts of heatwork have been achieved). When all was done, the fireboxes were sealed and the workers had all Sunday to recover, before returning to work on Monday: unpacking day. And so the rhythm went on. It seems to have been the norm to finish the week with a Friday firing in many potteries, the workers might get off work early on a Saturday, and of course the generous employer did not have to pay them on Sunday.

Some of the Buckley potters (e.g. Hayes) also used downdraught kilns incorporating clay drying pans. Perhaps they were influenced by the kilns for firebrick production, since the Hancock and Catherall families owned both potteries and refractory brickworks, and both were involved in salt-glaze stoneware pottery production in parallel with the earthenware, mainly bottles for Irish whiskey distillers.

(ABOVE) Mr. Button's kiln firing at Soil Hill. *Photograph by R. Fournier.*

(BELOW) Autumn 1964, one of the last firings at Soil Hill Pottery. *Photograph by J. Anderson.*

CHAPTER TEN

Kïln Setting

WHATEVER ITS DESIGN, IT has always been a skilled job to pack or 'set' the pots in the kiln to get reliable results. Big pots must be protected from too direct a flame, and certain areas of the kiln would need more open or tight packing to encourage the even distribution of heat. Other areas would inevitably be cold spots, and had to be filled up with flowerpots which, being unglazed, would still be saleable even when fired at a slightly lower temperature. If there was no specialist, it would fall to a senior member of the pottery team to set the kiln, for the outcome affected everybody's earnings. Usually, he would have an apprentice or two to do the fetching and carrying.

Packing the kiln at Crossroads Pottery, Verwood

In the Verwood style kiln, as can be seen (see photograph on p. 100) the pans were inverted one on another, built up layer by layer. The internal glaze was quite thin and it stopped short of the rim. On the floor of the kiln, nests of pans could be set, the larger ones over smaller sizes like a series of bases of Russian dolls. Higher in the pack this was less possible, but smaller jugs or cups could be put on the base of a pan and covered like a saggar by the next pan to be set. Each pan bridged two on the previous layer; one can often see on the bases two or three arcs where the next layer of them was fired. If one imagines the pans in plan, where three circular pots are packed tightly together there is a triangular space. In each such space a bottle or jug could be suspended, supported upside-down and touching at three points. The glaze on the narrower neck had no risk of touching, and it was this method of firing them that dictated their shape. The light coloured clay shows the flame path by reduction flashing, and pale shadows where another pot has been in contact with it, sheltering it from the flames. A piece of clay or two would be enough to stabilise any unsteady pots, so that there was no movement. Later in the packing, bats would be put on the bases of the upturned pans, and bridged by short boards to support the weight of the packer as he built up the layers. Glazed dishes and bread-crock lids would be fired on their rims, supported by a shard and leaning against the kiln wall or another pot. The pack would be completed from the top of the wall, and topped off with two or three layers of large shards, each layer bridging the gaps between the previous layer.

Packing the Wrecclesham bottle kiln

The packing of the bottle kiln at Wrecclesham was also undertaken with no shelves as such, although bricks were built up in openwork walls in a chequer pattern, and bridged every 3 ft or so, so the weight of the higher part of the pack was borne by the bricks rather than the ware. The larger flowerpots had a thrown ring a few inches high placed on the base, then the next upturned pot, and so on to form a stack 2 to 3 ft high. Stacks of Fred Whitbread's

(OPPOSITE PAGE) Packing day at Poling Pottery. This two-firebox bottle kiln seems to have been used as a top-up for the main production kiln, and would have been fired occasionally.

small pots filled every space between the larger ones, as well as inside any larger pots at the top of stacks or otherwise open to the atmosphere.

Since the chamber was round, setting was in concentric rings, starting at the outside and working in. Inside the circular bagwall, a ring of stacks of

(ABOVE) The master, Mesheck Sims, sets the unfired wares in the kiln. Len Sims passes-in, and the lad, Harold Churchill, does the leg work fetching pots from the workshop and bringing them to the top of the mound. *Photograph from The Verwood Historical Society.*

(RIGHT) Verwood potters climbing the shard-strewn kiln mound with the raw pots to be packed. The kiln still has a temporary planked roof, later replaced by corrugated iron sheets. *Photograph from The Verwood and District Potteries Trust archive.*

Beginning to draw the kiln after firing. Although a lot has already been removed, and the top layer of vases has been placed on the setting for the picture, the pans and sideways jugs have not yet been disturbed. Potters; H. Bailey, M. Sims, L. Sims and J. Scammel. *Photograph from The Verwood Historical Society.*

six medium-sized pots would be followed by a ring of fired bricks with gaps between them built up like a chequer. At this reduced circumference were a series of fireholes over which land drain pipes were placed to protect the pots. Then another chequer of bricks, another ring of pots and so on into the centre, and the packer found himself in a narrow well. At the height of about 3 ft, the long specially made extruded bricks, some of them cut into wedge shapes, would be used to bridge the concentric chequer walls in a radial fashion.

At this stage, larger pots can be set, again surrounded by stacks of small pots. Boards to stand on while packing the next level are placed on an inner circle of radial bricks, again starting with the peripheral circles and working in, bringing the setting to the top of the bagwall. Stacks of small pots are used for the outer circles, now touching the wall, and as the circumference decreases toward the centre the pots increase in size, with large strawberry pots and large planters near the middle. And so

another layer is formed, bringing the concentric stacks to a uniform height, and finally the whole setting is covered with loosely set pan tiles. These tiles have the same function as the shards topping-off the Verwood style kiln. They prevent 'chimneys' occuring where the heat would escape too directly without filtering evenly through the ware. They also keep the heat in, and act like the perforated dome of a slightly more sophisticated kiln.

Kiln setting was finished off from the 'wicket' door, before blocking it with three courses of loosely-set bricks, the outer one clammed with the usual sloppy mixture of clay and sand. The full setting of this kiln, the last big bottle kiln to be used in England, would be about 12 ft high.

Packing with pan-rings

When packing a bottle or downdraught kiln, using pan rings (see photograph on p. 103) in order to

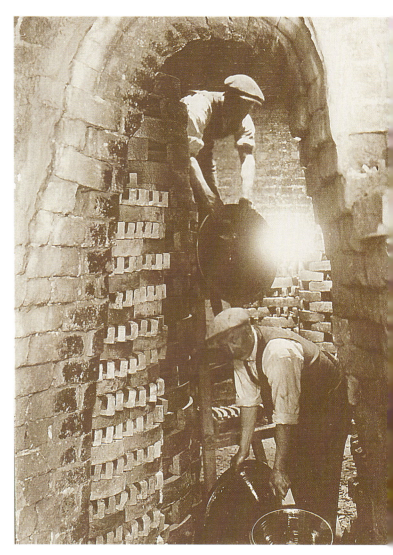

Inside the bottle kiln at Wrecclesham during packing. From the central well of loose-built bricks, the specially made radial bricks support the strawberry pots. Behind, the outer stacks of small pots are already complete, and topped with their layer of pantiles. Above these, the chalkline to show the course of brick used in the firing to gauge the level of the setting. *Photograph by Andrew Holloway.*

Unpacking pancheons at Lamb's Pottery in Buckley, 1909. Inside the 'wicket', a stack of smaller pan rings, then a bung of large ones, from the top of which the potter on the step-ladder is passing down pots, then a set of pan rings alternately.

make best use of the space, the largest pancheons were set on the outermost circle. The big 24 in. wash pans were set in 5 in. pan rings, while for pans of less than 12 in. diameter, smaller 3 in. pan rings were used. While usually pan rings are 'L' sectioned with right angled corners, some of those used at Wetheriggs, whilst retaining the right angles on the outside, had a curve on the interior, the part which was in contact with the rim of the pan (pancheon). This would facilitate a straight and even movement downward, as the pan shrank in the ring. Shrinkage

is slight, even in large pots; this is a major difference between earthenware kiln setting compared to setting a stoneware firing where shrinkage is much greater.

Pans hang in the pan rings the right way up, but in south Wales and north Devon, in their updraught kilns, they set them upside down and were therefore obliged to have pans with unglazed

(OPPOSITE PAGE) The beginning of a bung of pancheons in the kiln at Soil Hill, 1964. *Photograph by J. Anderson.*

rims. In this way they were more sure that the heat would enter and penetrate each pan. In Buckley and at Wetheriggs the stacks of pans were up to 60 high; the whole height of the setting.

A pile of saggars, or a stack of pancheons in their pan rings is known as a 'bung'. A bung of twenty-five 24 in. pans gave a height of 6 ft, which was topped-off with a 'piecrust' or larger 'panbrim', that is, a circular slab of fireclay, usually with a hole in the middle, which would be stacked to the arch

(ABOVE) Stoking the bavins at the Crossroads kiln. Pans are stacked in the stoking shed to dry with the residual heat of the kiln after a firing. The kiln is not really being fired; this was a bit of play-acting by potter Fred Fry for a five minute film made in 1917 by Charles Urban about the pottery, now in the National Film Archive. See also p. 96. *Photograph from The Verwood and District Potteries Trust archive.*

(LEFT) Pans of the type made in south Wales and north Devon, fired rim downward in the panrings. Difference in temperature and atmosphere in the firing has given varied colouration.

During packing at Soil Hill, 1964. *Photograph by J. Anderson.*

with flowerpots. Any gaps between bungs of pans would be filled with stacks of flowerpots.

Packing the upright pots

More upright pots, like the tall milk pots of Buckley, or the tall lidless jars from Burton in Lonsdale, were stacked rim to rim, separated by wads made from sandy fireclay. Jugs and other closed-in forms, if only glazed to the shoulder or rim, were often fired on their side, and small ones were suspended among other unglazed wares as at Verwood. It is easy to see at what angle pots were fired, by the drips or traces of iron-rich glaze where the colouring has been absorbed as the glaze has flowed across a grain of iron-bearing sand.

Fine wares had always been fired using saggars with holes in their walls, and it was not until the introduction of refractory slabs and shelves that jugs and crocks with more fully glazed exteriors could be produced. It was only by supporting each pot separately on kiln shelves that a pot too large to be fired in a saggar could be fired without the risk of touching its neighbours. Richard Warner, at the end of the 18th century, mentioned the use of fireclay saggars and 'pot blocks' (probably pan rings) at Buckley. The home-made slabs and shelves as used by Mr Button at Soil Hill were made to last, and were often 3 or 4 in. thick. Because of the inconvenience of their weight they were sometimes set permanently in the kiln, as at Wetheriggs where they are set round the periphery of the chamber, with only the bung by the door to be built up at each firing. The previously mentioned 'pie crust' or 'panbrim' was also used as an intermediate form of shelving. Isaac Button would put fireclay wads round the rim of a breadcrock, for example, set a piecrust on top, and a stew pot on top of that, to fill the space to the next thick shelf (see photograph).

One item that was particularly difficult to pack in the kiln was the cloam oven, especially the larger sizes. As, in the updraught kilns, the gentlest heat was at the top, the ovens had to be lifted to the top of the setting, sometimes by several men. Unpacking them from a still warm kiln was not much easier.

CHAPTER ELEVEN

Distribution and Sale

THE FINAL PART OF ANY potter's job is to market his wares. There were various options: selling direct to customers who came to the pottery, or through a regular market stall or shop. Otherwise potters could wholesale to shops or other retailers, or to the hawkers and gypsies who sold door to door, calling on farms and hamlets throughout the countryside. The majority of sales were wholesale, selling the wares by the cast.

Memories of a Buckley pot seller

Adrian Childs interviewed probably the last Buckley pot seller for his oral history project of 1994 at Harlech College. Dorothy Ann Evans is from a gypsy family who had dealt in Buckley wares for generations. From about 1930 until the end of the potteries, just after the Second World War, she would regularly visit the two remaining potteries. Hayes Pottery closed in 1942, while Lambs tried restarting after the war, but found it no longer possible to get raw materials from their traditional suppliers. They too gave up just after the war. Another contributing factor to the closure was a change in the regulations concerning milk storage. Farmers were obliged to install stainless steel tanks, and at a stroke there was no demand for one of the main products of the Buckley potteries, the talk milk pots.

Here are some extracts from the tape recorded interviews between Adrian Childs and Mrs Evans.

Q. What type of pots did you buy?
A. Well, we used to have the milk pots, the big

Packing the pony and trap at Verwood. The boy hands up a 'Dorset owl'. *Photograph from The Verwood and District Potteries Trust archive.*

ones; they used to call them 'piece pots'. (Then) there was two in a piece; they were 'half pieces'. Then there were four in a piece . . . Then there would be pan-mugs, the same as those; piece pan-mugs and half-piece pan-mugs. Then there was the little pots, milk pots those were, eight in a piece – were only a little one, eight in a piece. I can remember that there (were) some dishes to make pudding in, they were 18 ... in a piece. Then there were smaller ones again, 24 in a piece; and the last ones of all were only like little bowls, 30 in a piece.

Buckley dish. With a flat base and short upright wall, these dishes could hold their shape, and so could be turned off their wooden humpmould a few minutes after being formed.

Oval Buckley ham pan with a pair of handles at either end, and made by the 'leaf' method; 'the size of a baby's bath'.

Q. Do you remember; how much did you pay a piece?

A. I think they were very cheap then you know . . . They used to cost about 10 shilling; it all depends what was in them (there were some) for a pound a piece, but there was no more (expensive). You would have a load on the pony and cart for about six quid.

Q. Where did you sell them?

A. Around the farms.

Q. The farms in the area?

A. Wherever we was; Use'to be in Llansanhan, Denbigh, Pwllheli, Corwen, Bala ... all around.

Dorothy Hartley described visiting one of the Buckley potteries, probably Hayes, in the 1930s where she would go to buy pots for her own use.

> The output is largely of plain round bowls, wash basin shape, so much used in the district, deep bread panshions ... and milk pudding dishes. They make also a fair number of wine jars ... Sometimes there will be half a dozen large oval panshions the size of a baby's bath, for curing hams; sometimes rows of deep handled pots that we use for bailing jam or fruit messes. Another time there will be a kiln full of hotpots. Once there was a kiln full of pottery spittoons for public houses: another

time they concentrated on jugs, ... (or on) heavy bread pans and jars ... As a rule each kiln is packed with more or less the same things.

The Wetheriggs 'potters'

Wetheriggs pots were also often sold through the travelling folk, who were often referred to as 'potters', that is to say, pot sellers. The nearby Appleby horse fair was always a gathering point in the gypsies' annual travels. Harold Thorburn (1916–1960) of Wetheriggs remembered. One of the first customers he had to deal with when he was first employed by Arthur Schofield was one of these 'potter cart men' passing on his way from the fair. The gypsy was able to buy a full load for the pony and cart for 10 shillings, including a good proportion of seconds.

The Verwood 'higglers'

The hawkers who sold the Verwood wares, by contrast, were usually members of the potter's (maker's) families. Another name by which they were known was a 'higgler' (higgle means the same as haggle). They, like the gypsies, would have their regular rounds to farms, villages and private houses.

(TOP) 'Pans' Brewer in his prime shortly after the First World War, walking the Dorset lanes with Verwood pots for sale.
Photograph from The Verwood Historical Society.

(ABOVE) Progress. Mr. Brewer, still in business in the 1940s, now with Mr. King to drive him on his rounds.
Photograph from The Verwood Historical Society.

In the stockroom at Soil Hill, 1962. *Photograph by J. Anderson.*

As well as the pots, they also sold besom brooms, another local heathland product. One of the last of these was 'Pans' Brewer, or 'Brush' Brewer, a relation of the potter 'Drummer' Brewer seen in the photographs on p. 92. By the 1940s, the horse and cart had gone, and he had to get someone to drive him, like Mr King (see photograph on p. 108). In spite of this shift of technology, the old Mr Brewer could not help himself from talking to the driver as if he was a horse, with commands like 'Woah there' and 'Steady'.

Transport

It seems the coming of canal, and later rail, transport helped the industrial potters rather than the country variety. High weight and low value meant the cost and trouble of packing and transporting the wares in these ways was uneconomical in most cases. Fremington Pottery occasionally packed a railway waggon of cloam ovens for Cornwall, and at Wetheriggs, which had a branch-line nearby, pots were sometimes despatched packed in straw in hazelwood crates by train. Horse and cart remained the means of transport most suited to the needs of potteries well into the 20th century, and its demise more or less corresponded with that of the potteries.

Before the coming of the railways, some centres of pottery production which were on or near the coast had access to transport by sea. Fremington and Bideford, Ewenny and Buckley could all benefit from proximity to the thriving coastal traders. The schooners, brigs and sloops used varied in size from 40 to 150 tons. Many shipments of Buckley pots went off to Dublin, as well as to smaller Welsh ports. The north Devon potters could get their coal from south Wales, and send pots in the opposite direction.

In the mid-19th century William Catherall did an annual tour of Ireland to visit customers, taking orders and collecting debts. He also regularly visited wholesale customers throughout Wales.

Map of
old country pottery sites
mentioned in text

Aberdeen (Seaton)

SCOTLAND

Glasgow   Edinburgh

Cumnock
Drongan

Newcastle-upon-Tyne

Penrith
(Wetheriggs)

Kirby Lonsdale

Ripon
(Littlethorpe)

(Soil Hill)
Halifax

Macclesfield
(Sutton)

Buckley   Stoke-on-Trent

WALES   ENGLAND

Ewenny
(also Claypits)   Winchcombe
Nettlebed
Cardiff   Reading
Luckington   (Colliers)
Barnstaple   London
(Brannams)   Farnborough
Farnham (Wrecclesham)
Fremington
Bideford   Dicker
Verwood   Fareham
(Crossroads)   Arundel
(Poling)

Truro (Lakes)

Potteries near large centres of population, too, had a marketing advantage. Ewenny pots were sold in the coal mining valleys, as well as in industrial Newport and Cardiff. Glasgow had several potteries around it, including those at Westbank and Rosebank. Newcastle had several potteries nearby including Isaac Wright's pottery at Ouseburn. Halifax and the industrial West Riding towns also had several potteries close by. Smith's pottery at Farnborough employed a carter to take the wares up to London, mostly to Whitechapel. The pots were packed in bracken directly in the cart, and piled 'two feet higher than the raves' (edge rails) and tied down with 'withies' (willow).

Markets and secondary produce

The Fishleys of Fremington had a regular stall each Friday at Barnstaple. When the Rodgers family worked the pottery at Donyatt they had a Saturday stall at Taunton. Later, when the Aldridges took over the pottery they had a permanent shop there.

Wasters and cinders were sold to local farmers for roadmaking. Wetheriggs similarly sold the stones washed out of the clay, as well as cinders. Another secondary form of income was agricultural produce. If the potter owned some land where the clay pit was, and the horse had to be pastured somewhere, it was only a small step to keep a cow, fatten a pig, keep some poultry and so on.

William Smith very much saw himself as both farmer and potter. At Fremington they grew corn and mangels for the horse, potatoes for the family and pigs. They also tended a large garden, the excess produce from which they sold wholesale, presumably to a fellow market-stall holder. It may have been the importance of some of the Verwood potters' farming activities that limited their technical progress. For many, pottery seems to have been a seasonal activity.

CHAPTER TWELVE

In the Footsteps of the Country Potters

THERE ARE NO PEASANTS left in Britain and therefore no demand for the artefacts that were part of that culture. There is a small minority who by choice make bread and store it in a bread-crock, but to buy a handmade pot is no longer the cheapest option; it has to be a conscious decision. So the role of the handmade pots is inevitably different to what went before, but that does not mean the influence of traditional pots and ways of working have disappeared or have been forgotten. Tradition was always fluid, never static; with each generation it is reinterpreted and reinvented. If anyone should doubt that the craft skills are as good as they were in the old days, they should visit some of the potters listed in this chapter. They are all people who make a living by their craft. If their work is 'conservative', their aim is to make a practical, functioning craft object rather than a piece of 'original' art (if such a thing exists). If the pots are of a personal style and have originality, that is secondary to their function.

On the other hand the country potters, as well as making traditional forms, also made decorative wares, which were not necessarily of the same level of spontaneity and skill. In short, not all the old pots were good, and not all the contemporary ones are bad. At any period, the potter of functional wares must tread a careful path between function and demand for novelty, and the constraints of making a living. Although a potter like Mr Button was working within a tradition, his pots are quite recognisably his, and it was the same for any country potter; although individual style became blurred into a workshop style when they worked as a team. The same applies to Ray Finch today. I would encourage people to enjoy what is available today, rather than dwell on what has alrady gone, although to understand where we have come from might inform us about what direction to take in the future.

Traces of the past

What remains of the old potteries? Most have been destroyed or redeveloped. At Rye Pottery in Sussex and at Ewenny, pots of a decorative nature continue to be made, developing the 'art ware' style rather than country pots. Brannams buildings were redeveloped as housing, but the firm, no longer owned by the family, continues to produce mostly pressed flowerpots at a new factory site on the edge of Barnstaple, as well as being importers of gardenware from the Far East. Other old potteries have survived on the same site by changing with the times, and adapting to the changing market in their own ways; these will be listed amongst more recently established works.

Sometimes only remnants remain: houses, workshops adapted for other uses, the odd bottle kiln standing isolated at Nettlebed in Oxfordshire, or that of the estate pottery at Luckington, for example. There are several pottery sites in and around Verwood, all privately owned, but all the kilns have been stripped of their brick linings so that they remain only as bramble-covered mounds.

Only the house and bottle kiln remain at Luckington near Bath. The occupants of the house try to disguise the huge kiln in their garden by growing a creeper up it.

The Crossroads pottery at Verwood, where the photographs were taken, remains surprisingly unchanged, although the kiln was destroyed and replaced by a bungalow. Efforts to preserve the site have not met with great success and it is under threat of demolition. Another long running saga in similar vein is that of Soil Hill, the buildings of which continue to deteriorate. The Farnham Pottery at Wrecclesham has been bought by the Farnham Buildings Preservation Trust who have serious structural problems to deal with before the site can be reopened. Members of the Harris family may in the future lease part of the building for pottery production. The land attached to the pottery has been sold and used for housing.

At the Museum of Welsh Life at St Fagans a kiln and pottery building from Ewenny have been recreated where, as at Wetheriggs, children can attempt to throw a pot. There is also a small display of Ewenny pots, mostly decorative ware.

Although Littlethorpe and Winchcombe are still working potteries, Wetheriggs Pottery (see photograph on p. 123) is unique in being the only working pottery plus museum. Since the days of the traditional potters, successive owners have done much to restore and preserve this old works, notably Jonathan Snell, and the present owner Bill Dodd. Perhaps one day, some of the other country potteries may restart as working museums, but for the moment, Wetheriggs is on its own.

The tradition evolves

A former tradition cannot be revived; to make pots the same as the old ones is to make 'reproductions'. What one makes must to some extent suit the society one lives in, or appeal to a large enough minority to sell enough to make a living. Many potters admire country pots without their work being directly influenced by them. The selection of potters which follows are some whose pots and ways of working are, in their individual ways, following in the footsteps of the country potters. In the pursuit of equality and thoroughness I would have liked to have found potters in Scotland and Wales, and workshops led by women which fitted the criteria, but failed. The list is incomplete, and I apologise to those I have missed, but present day country potters like those in the past tend to be getting on with their work in rural isolation, and are not necessarily known to a public outside their own region. There are many women potters working within the teams of potters, particularly in the bigger workshops. The potters are of all ages, happily younger ones continue to set up workshops despite discouragement from the art schools and the art 'establishment' in general. The potters or potteries are listed in alphabetical order:

1   Svend Bayer
2   Clive Bowen
3   Richard Charters
4   Roland Curtis
5   Peter and Jill Dick
6   Bill Donaldson
7   Edmonds Brothers
8   Errington Reay & Co Ltd
9   Ray Finch at Winchcombe
10 Jonathan Garrat
11 John Huggins
12 Jonathan and Melanie Hughes-Jones
13 Jim Keeling
14 John Leach
15 Mick Pinner
16 Arnold Rose
17 Peter Strong at Wetheriggs
18 Mark Titchener

Svend Bayer, Duckpool Cottage, Sheepwash, Beaworthy, Devon EX21 5PW

After training with Michael Cardew, Svend (b. 1946) spent five months as thrower at Brannams of Barnstaple and some time visiting potteries in the Far East. Established in 1975, the pottery has had several large wood-fired kilns over the years, all Oriental crossdraught designs. All the pots are stoneware, with a mixed economy of both flowerpots and domestic

Jugs and bottles drying in Svend Bayer's pottery.
Photograph by Chris Chapman.

ware. The flowerpots are stacked rim to rim in the kiln, and made by throwing up added coils joined to the stiffened pot. The jugs are a continuation of the shapes made at Fremington, and like all the ware, once-fired. Until recently he has been working with an 800 cu. ft kiln but, with a change of emphasis to more domestic ware production, now uses a 150 cu. ft kiln which can be filled and fired once a month.

Clive Bowen, Shebbear Pottery, Beaworthy, Devon EX21 8QZ

Using Fremington clay from Brannams, 20 miles away, Clive (b. 1943) has been producing slip-decorated earthenware at the pottery since 1971. After an art school training, he spent four years at Yelland Pottery, and a year as thrower at Brannams. The kiln has two round wood-fired chambers, each

Unpacking the round kiln chamber at Shebbear Pottery, packed with bungs of saggars as well as shelves.
Photograph by C. Boursnell.

Big ware drying in the sun at Harehope Forge Pottery.
Photograph by R. Charters.

400 cu. ft. The first is downdraught, which pre-heats the second chamber: an updraught bottle kiln. Usually only the first chamber is used and fired with a range of raw-glazed domestic pots as well as unglazed flowerpots six or seven times a year. There are also wall tiles extruded from Fishley-Holland's old chain-drive pugmill. In the year, the pottery team varies in number between two and four people. On firing days, as well as other friends and helpers, Svend Bayer comes to help, on a reciprocal basis.

Richard Charters, Harehope Forge Pottery, Harehope Farm, Eglingham, Alnwick, Northumberland NE66 2DW

After art school at Farnham, Richard (b. 1962) went to all the right places. After three years at Wrecclesham, he worked for two years at Bardon Mill. Having set up the present workshop in 1991, he continues to produce a range of unglazed garden pots, which are wood-fired in a 170 cu. ft crossdraught kiln to 1020°C. Firings are once every four to six weeks, and sometimes take 30 hours. Clay comes from a brickworks ready prepared on pallets, 10 tons at a time. It is kept damp and, when required, a batch of half a ton is wedged by foot then finally hand-wedged in small amounts. The ware is thrown on a home-made momentum wheel.

Roland Curtis, Littlethorpe Pottery, Littlethorpe, Rippon, North Yorkshire HG4 3LS

George Curtis, when he was taken on at the pottery as clayboy in 1920, was part of a team of 19 men.

Decorative pancheon flowerpots by R. Curtis.

Peter and Jill Dick decorating ware. *Photograph by Tessa Bunney.*

He saw the trade dwindle through the years, and eventually ended up owning the place and working on his own. Apart from a brief spell when he tried turning the place into a chicken farm, he continued to produce wares, eventually dropping production of pancheons, stew pots and bread-crocks in favour of unglazed flowerpots.

'Roly' Curtis learnt the trade from his father, and continues to dig clay on site, prepare it with the big cast-iron barrelled pugmill, and throw it on a belt-drive cone (Boulton) wheel. Since the 1960s, an electric kiln has replaced the coal-fired kiln, but pigeon nests, flowerpots and various big wares continue to be produced and lifted off with the stick across the forearms in the same old way. Most of the ware is sold direct from the pottery. In the pottery shop there is a small museum display with some old equipment including a hand-cranked wheel. Littlethorpe remains perhaps the best preserved old pottery works which continues to function, with little of the fabric of the buildings having changed ... so far.

Peter and Jill Dick, Coxwold Pottery, Coxwold, York YO6 4AA

Long time admirers of the qualities of traditional earthenware, Peter and Jill often visited Isaac Button at Soil Hill in the 1960s. He even asked them if they were interested in buying the pottery when he retired. Unfortunately for the Soil Hill site, they declined, and set up their workshop in the beautiful village of Coxwold where they have worked ever since. Peter (b. 1936) and Jill (b. 1942) now work mainly on their own, with two part-time assistants. Most of the work is slip-decorated earthenware, with occasional batches of flowerpots and stoneware. Most of the pots are fired in small gas or electric kilns, and sold direct from the pottery shop. For many years they worked with several assistants, and fired the 160 cu. ft wood-kiln once a month. Over the years, the emphasis of the work has shifted towards more decorative work. Peter trained with Michael Cardew, and also worked for a while with Ray Finch at Winchcombe. Most of the ware is thrown, apart from a few press-moulded pie dishes, and fired to 1080°C (1976°F).

Bill Donaldson, Willow Pottery, Tog Hill House Farm, Freezing Hill, Wick, Nr Bath, Avon

Bill (b. 1953) and his wife Kim make flowerpots with a team of eight people, some of whom work part-time. Using 5 tonnes of clay per week, one of the 150 cu. ft kilns is fired every day. They use a high-firing red clay from Valentine's in Stoke-on-Trent which is very resistant to the risk of frost-

The pottery yard at Willow Pottery.

Freshly thrown pots at Tydd Pottery.
Photograph from Tydd Pottery.

damage. The business has grown over the years, and at the time of writing they are moving production to a new site: old farm buildings a few miles from the previous pottery, which they have outgrown. As well as showing their range of plain and decorative flowerpots at major garden shows, Chelsea, Hampton Court etc., they export container-loads of their wares abroad. One of the benefits of the new works is that they will be able to sell more pottery direct to the public.

John and Antony Edmonds, Tydd Pottery, Tydd Road, Pode Hole, Spalding, Lincolnshire PE11 3QA

Brothers Ant and John (b. 1944) have been making flowerpots together for 25 years. Self-taught, when they were starting they used to visit George Curtis at Littlethorpe quite often. The oil-fired 400 cu. ft kiln is fired roughly every three weeks. It takes 40 hours to

fire, and is left to cool for two days. They get through about 60 tonnes of Valentine's clay per year, and waste is recycled using long troughs lined with nylon cloth which hold about a ton each. The ware is sold direct from the pottery (Spalding is well known for bulb growing), as well as at garden shows, craft shows, and garden centres. Each of the brothers has their own shapes that they throw, and they both make big ware in two or sometimes three sections.

Errington Reay & Co Ltd, Tyneside Pottery Works, Bardon Mill, Hexham, Northumberland NE47 7HU

The salt-glazed stoneware pots from Bardon Mill are unique. The range of ware includes bread-crocks and large storage jars as well as a wide range of flowerpots, including various shapes and sizes of strawberry pot. In the mid-1970s the previous owners found themselves with an extruded drainage-pipe factory (est. 1878) whose market had faded away with the increasing encroachment of plastic pipes. With the help of Harrow-trained* potter Steve Course,

* Many contemporary professional potters trained at what was then called Harrow College of Higher Education in the 1960s and 1970s. One of the course leaders was Michael Casson (see preface).

they transformed the works into a pottery, retaining the use of the local fireclay, the clay plant and vertical extruders and the 1000 cu. ft round downdraught coal-fired kiln.

A piece of extrusion is flattened on a bat to make the base of a pot, and to this a cylindrical extrusion is joined. Centred on the wheel, the rim of stiff clay is turned over, and the wall swelled out. A deft bit of combing, a pair of pulled handles, and the pot is finished. The pottery employs 10 people, and firings are once a week.

Pipeworks like this were established on the coal measures, where the associated fireclays could be used in the extrusion machines developed in the mid-19th century. As well as pipes, they produced kitchen sinks, animal feed troughs, garden edging, chimney pots, and sometimes even garden furniture. Pipeworks were widespread in the lowlands of Scotland, and in the north and the Midlands of England, as well as on the south coast, where they found the ball clays round Poole suitable for the process.

The semi-automated making process is ideal for producing large quantities of simple and cheap pots (if slightly limited in form). In the yard, half-priced seconds wait in stacks for customers; the garden centres who buy wholesale do not accept pots with drips from the dome of the kiln, or other faults like too much orange-peel texture.

Ray Finch, Winchcombe Pottery, Winchcombe, Nr Cheltenham, Gloucestershire GL54 5NU

Ray Finch (b. 1914) joined Cardew's team at the pottery in 1936. He is still active in the pottery team, although managing the pottery has passed to one of his sons, Mick Finch (b. 1946) since Ray's 'official' retirement some years ago. Eddy Hopkins is the main thrower in a team of five potters. The story of this old traditional pottery has already been told elsewhere (see bibliography). Earthenware production ended in the 1950s, to be succeeded by stoneware. The 130 cu. ft wood-kiln is fired every three or four weeks, and a 25 cu. ft gas-fired salt-kiln every eight weeks. The practical domestic ware is integrity in pottery form. Prices are kept deliberately low, and the range of wares includes bread-crocks, cider jars with spiggots, mugs, bowls, plates etc. Some surfaces are left

The stockyard at Bardon Mill. The dome kiln chamber is between chimney stack and workshops.

The old horse-drawn pugmill behind the pottery at Winchcombe has not been used since they gave up earthenware production.

unglazed to be 'flashed' by the wood-firing, and other pots are entirely glazed in a range of glazes, often used over combed slip decoration; this decoration is entirely their own, but one can see a familial connection with the slip-combing of Fremington.

Jonathan Garratt, Hare Lane Pottery, Cranborne, Dorset BH21 5QT

Not far from Verwood, Jonathan (b. 1954) uses clay he gets from a local farmer. After weathering, it is blunged in an old hexagonal blunger powered by a diesel engine. After passing through a sieve, it is run out into drying pans and air dried to a plastic state in a long shed. The round-chambered down-draught wood-kiln (250 cu. ft) is fired about once every six weeks; the firing takes 17 hours. The ware, all high-fired earthenware, includes a range of plain and decorative flowerpots, as well as some slipped and glazed domestic ware. His speciality is the decorative garden ware, which is often textured with rouletting.

John Huggins between his dough mixer and blunger.

The kiln room from the pottery yard at Hare Lane Pottery.

John Huggins, Ruardean Garden Pottery, Ruardean, Forest of Dean, Gloucestershire GL17 9TP

John Huggins (b. 1954) has been making flowerpots professionally since 1979. He works with a small team: his wife, an assistant learning the trade, and one full-time thrower. John trained at the famous Harrow course for potters. The clay comes from various local brickworks – from one industrial brickworks in the form of pallets of unfired brick (see photograph). Clays are blended in the blunger, then filter-pressed. A wide range of flowerpots is produced, including rhubarb and seakale forcers, plain flowerpots and ones decorated with simple stamped designs. The clay is pushed from inside the pot into the clay or plaster decorative mould. Although the majority of the pots are thrown, there is also a range of press-moulded ware: oval and

'Long Tom' tall flowerpots, rhubarb forcer and pancheons at Pembridge.

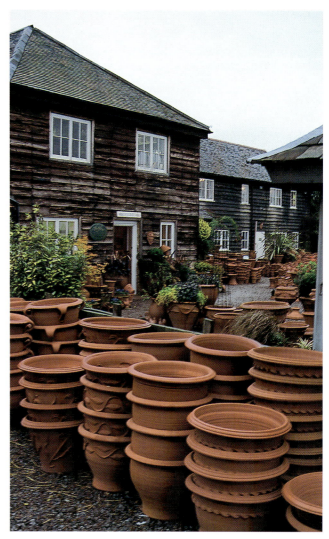

Whichford Pottery from the stockyard.

square planters, and some large octagonal ones. Garden ornaments are also part of the range, some of which are made by slipcasting.

Jonathan & Melanie Hughes-Jones, Pembridge Terracotta, Pembridge, Herefordshire HR6 9HB

Melanie and Jonathan, both Harrow-trained potters, have a most picturesque, if cramped, workshop in the High Street of the black and white timber-framed village of Pembridge. After having been side-tracked into the manufacture of pottery doorknobs for some years, they have returned to potting in a big way. The team of five or six potters produce a full range of thrown flowerpots, as well as a small amount of glazed ware. Their clay is provided by a local farmer, and the 100 cu. ft gas kiln is fired at least three times a week. It is a fixed-hearth trolley-chamber fibre kiln, and above it is a slatted floor where pots are given a final drying before descending to the ground floor by

lift for firing. The pots have generous forms and robust rims. Like the other bigger flowerpot works, they export container-loads of ware. They are also able to sell a good proportion direct to customers, as one of the main routes into Wales passes their door.

Jim Keeling, Whichford Pottery, Whichford, Shipston-on-Stour, Warwickshire CV36 5PG

Whichford is the biggest producer of hand-made garden ware in Britain. The scale of production is impressive, the yard a sea of terracotta awaiting customers. Jim (b. 1952) trained at Wrecclesham. The current workforce is 36 in number, including seven throwers, some of whom are self-employed and only come in two or three days per week, and

The pottery team c. 1985; Ivan Bingham, John Leach, and Nick Rees. *Photograph by R.J. Whittick.*

work elsewhere the rest of the week. Several people make press-moulded pots and garden ornaments, others decorate, sprig and handle pots. Some prepare the clay. The blend of two local clays is blunged and filter-pressed in a 2.5 tonne filter-press. Four mixes a week are passed through a large de-airing pugmill, with the addition of some fine silver sand, to give the required 10 tonnes per week. A pair of 140 cu. ft fibre trolley kilns run more or less continually (there is also a third slightly smaller kiln) providing drying upstairs in the slatted-floored drying room. There is also a dehumidifying chamber: a sort of insulated room where a machine draws in air, and condenses the water from it, somewhat on the same lines as the workings of a refrigerator. Much of the ware is large in scale. When I last visited, one thrower was making 56

pounders, while the chief thrower Tony Hall was joining and finishing the top sections of some two-part 100 lb pots. The largest 'Ali Baba' jars are made in three sections, but most of the ware bigger than 60 lbs is thrown in two sections. Experimentation in new design and colour is constant. They also produce floor tiles and glazed wall tiles. Jim's wife Dominique also makes sgraffito-decorated glazed wares. Whichford Pottery serves as testimony to what can be achieved, given the will, personal commitment and entrepreneurial skill.

John Leach, Muchelney Pottery, Muchelney, Nr Langport, Somerset TA10 0DW

Third generation potter John Leach (b. 1939) is a grandfather himself these days. In spite of pressure

Mick Pinner's traditional chimney pots.

The drying rack at Arnold Rose's Brighton workshop.
Photo from Brighton Evening Argus.

to make 'art', he has consistently produced a range of robust functional stoneware since establishing the pottery in 1964. The unglazed exteriors of jugs, dishes and casseroles are 'flashed' by the flame and ash in the 350 cu. ft three-chambered wood-kiln, which fires six times a year. Apart from training in the family workshops, John spent some time working with Colin Pearson and at Winchcombe. He works with the help of his wife Elizabeth and two or three assistants, including long-term colleague Nick Rees. The simple practical pots continue the English tradition; one might say he practices what his grandfather Bernard preached.

Mick Pinner, West Meon Pottery, Lippen Hill, Church Lane, West Meon, Petersfield, Hampshire GU32 1JW

Mick Pinner (b. 1960) gets his clay from the local tile-works at Midhurst by the lorry-load. It weathers in the yard until required. After art school at Farnham, Mick worked at Wrecclesham (1982–84) and continues to prepare his clay in the old way: leaving it in a brick-lined soaking pit for 48 hours, then pugging. With the enormous 1950s pugmill,

he can extrude a ridge-tile including its upstanding part (to be decoratively cut at a later stage) off the 12 in. diameter end. As well as a range of generously thrown flowerpots and jars, some very big, he makes various architectural ceramics to order. This range of work includes chimney pots, medieval-style tiles, decorative ridge tiles, moulded special bricks and roof finials. The round (180 cu. ft) downdraught kiln, sometimes with a little salt to flash the pots, is fired once every month or so.

Arnold Rose, 5 Arundel Road, Brighton, East Sussex BN2 5TE

Tucked away in a mews behind the Bush public house, not far from the seafront, Harrow-trained Arnold Rose (b. 1956) with one assistant makes a good range of flowerpots and some glazed domestic ware. The clay is from the local Keymer tileworks. In spite of the urban setting, the well-thrown flowerpots have a vitality reminiscent of the work of the old country potters. Most of the work is thrown; sometimes the flowerpots have a decorative green-glazed rim. There are also some rectangular seed-pans and troughs. If the pots are decorated,

In the foreground, the restored sunpan at Wetheriggs Pottery.

this is mostly confined to sprigged masks of lions, green men, Tudor roses (of course) or grotesques. The pottery was started in 1987, and more recently expanded into further buildings in the mews.

Wetheriggs Country Pottery, Clifton Dykes, Penrith, Cumbria CA10 2DH

Preserved as a 'national industrial monument' since 1973, Wetheriggs has become more than just a pottery. Now owned by Bill Dodd and with Jo Chapman as director, the place is quite a hive of activity. There are several gift shops on the site, as well as a tea room, play areas, rare breed pigs, newt ponds etc. The old workshop with its long hypocaust dryers has become a museum, along with the beehive kiln, showing many examples of the old wares, as well as tools and equiment. The steam-engine has been restored, as well as the blunger and sunpans. There are several potters, making a wide range of wares from decorative slipwares to painted tin-glazed ware.

Peter Strong (b. 1952), who owned the pottery for a while, is also part of the team. After an art school training, Peter rented part of the Soil Hill Pottery for four years during the 1970s, making pots resembling those of Isaac Button. Now, years later these continue, sometimes using bright slips and leadless glazes, as well as a full range of terracotta garden pots. Although throwing is the main method of making, he also uses some multiple-part plaster moulds to press-mould Victorian style garden urns and statuary.

Mark Titchener, Chediston Pottery, Chediston Green, Halesworth, Suffolk IP19 0BB

Mark Titchener (b. 1953) is a plant pot maker who has more recently expanded his range of wares to include glazed domestic ware. The red clay is a mixture of Fremington clay and another from Burgess Hill in Sussex. Both are delivered 'as dug' into a sunpan. Sand is added when the stiffened clay is pugmilled. The wood-fired kiln, like that of Jonathan Garrett, was designed by Michael O'Brien. The round chamber is 8 ft across and 8 ft high; about 400 cu. ft. There are six firemouths, and the downdraught chamber is fired to around 1030°C (1886°F) to 1040°C (1904°F) in 30 hours, after a 16 hour warm-up, which preheats the pots to about 200°C (392°F). The present workshop was established in 1982.

Mark Tichener's round down-draught kiln chamber, with its high bagwall visible inside. *Photograph by M. Titchener.*

Glossary

Art ware or art pottery. Decorative ware of various and novel forms and decorations (often vases) made for the growing middle-classes in the period 1875 to 1920. As well as the handmade varieties made in country potteries, it was produced in factories some of which had a special art department where signed individual pieces were produced.

Bagwall. Small protective wall inside the kiln chamber opposite the entrance from the firebox. The bagwall space is the space within it, and by extension above it.

Bat. A removable wooden disc, usually stuck onto the wheel-head with a layer of clay, which allows the potter to remove the pot from the wheel without touching it. The bat acts as temporary false wheel-head. (The term kiln-bat is sometimes used instead of kiln shelf; the latter is used in this book in order to avoid confusion with the above).

Bavins. Another name for 'faggots', bundles of twiggy materials, often gorse bushes or hedge cuttings.

Biscuit. Fired unglazed pottery.

Blunge. To mix clay with water and agitate the mixture.

Bushel. Measure of capacity equivalent to 8 gallons or 32 quarts, often used when measuring grain, fruit, etc.

Bussas. This is the spelling Fishley-Holland used to describe what H. W. Strong called 'buzzards' in his 1889 'Industries of North Devon' (see bibliography for the reprint). These tall swelling jars had two vertical handles descending from a thick rim, like the wings of the hunched profile of a perched buzzard on a cold winter morning.

Clay winning. The process of digging the clay and bringing it back to the works.

Coarse ware. A somewhat derogatory description of pottery which is not 'fine' tableware. A term used by historians to describe functional earthenware pots.

Cob. A material for walls, made from clay and gravel, reinforced with straw.

Common redware. Generic term used by historians for red coloured pottery, usually earthenware.

Costrel. A small bottle used by travellers and harvesters, with two handles near the neck, so that it could be carried by a cord attached to them.

Delftware. Decorative tin-glazed earthenware made to resemble the expensive imported porcelain from China. The manufacture of Delft ware was introduced from Holland, where the city of Delft was a major centre of production.

Dorset owls. Costrels made at Verwood, whose round shape and two decorative handles on the shoulders gave them the appearance of the head of an owl (see p. 25 and p. 30).

Extruder. Machine with a barrel that can be charged with clay, which is then pushed by a plunger towards a die-plate, that is a metal plate with a hole in it which is the shape of the section of the pot. They were often used to produce land drains, and long or rectangular seed pans and flowerpots.

Firebars. Bars of metal or ceramic which support the burning fuel in the firebox. They allow more air to get to the fuel, while ash and embers fall to the floor.

Flywheel. The large wheel which provides momentum for a kickwheel, usually fixed low on the same shaft that has the wheel-head at the top.

Frit. Soluble or poisonous materials are often 'fritted' so that they can be more easily and safely used in glazes. The material, eg. lead is fired with silica in a special frit kiln until it fuses to form a glass. This glass or frit when cool is subsequently ground to a fine powder, which can then be combined with other materials to form a glaze.

Galena. Lead sulphide, a naturally occuring ore, sometimes referred to as 'blue lead'. Once ground to a powder it has a sparkling grey appearance. When fired to about 950°C (1742°F) it melts and fuses with the surface of the clay to form a shiny clear glaze. The sulphur part of the compound escapes during the firing in the form of gasses (see glazing p. 81).

Grog. Coarse material mixed with the clay to reduce shrinkage in drying and firing, so lessening the risk of cracking. Grog is often made by crushing fired clay to a powder but for the country potter, sand was a cheaper and easily available alternative.

Hypocaust. A hollow space under the floor, into which hot air is sent for heating a room. In the potteries these were in the form of flue-ways beneath racking.

Lute. To join together two parts of a pot, usually having scratched and slurried the surface to be joined.

Pan rings. Refractory supports used for pancheons in the kiln (see photographs on p. 103). Arc shaped; 'L' shaped in section, they were stacked up to form a tall cylindrical 'bung', with the rim of a pancheon supported by each circle of them. As the circle of pan rings left gaps, they allowed the heat and gasses to circulate during firing.

Peck. Measure of capacity of 2 gallons, otherwise 8 quarts or a $^1/_4$ bushel.

Porringers. Small bowl from which soup or porridge is eaten.

Profile. Small rib-like tool sometimes used to give decorative ridging or a standard profile, particularly for rims eg. on jam pots or bottles.

Pugmill. (See photographs on p. 39 and p. 44 –5). The pug-mill both mixes and compresses the clay. Once loaded into the barrel, the clay is cut and pushed by angled blades on a turning central shaft, before emerging from the other end of the barrel as an extrusion. Cut lengths of this extrusion were known as a 'pug' of clay, hence the name.

Puzzle jugs. Multiple-spouted hollow-handled jugs used in a drinking game. In order to drink without spillage one had to block all spouts and concealed holes, and suck on one of the spouts.

Quart. Measure of capacity of 2 pints, or a quarter of a gallon, or in metric, 1101 cc.

Racks. Means of supporting the boards of drying pots.

Refractory. Refractory clays (and other materials) are those resistant to high temperatures. Fireclay, found in proximity to coal seams, was the country potter's refractory.

Rib. Flat tool held in the throwers hand to smooth the surface of the pot in the later stages of throwing.

Rustic ware or rustic pottery. Items such as plant pots and tobacco jars were often textured with a fork to imitate the texture of bark. Cut branches were modelled and sometimes picked out in white slip for contrast. It is just one form of art ware, and corresponded with contemporary 'rustic' garden furniture, picture frames etc. in various materials which were similarly branch-like.

Saggar. Refractory box, often round or oval in plan, and cylindrical, used to contain small ware in the kiln firing.

Sgrafitto. A form of decoration made by scratching through slip on pottery, to show the colour of the clay beneath.

Slip. A clay or body mixed with water, until it has the consistency of double cream.

Slurry. The thick slip which accumulates in the potters wheeltray, not liquid enough to be called slip, nor firm enough to be workable clay.

Sour. 'Souring' or aging the clay happens naturally when the soft clay is stored. Plasticity is improved by the growth of bacteria between the microscopic plate-like particles of clay. Before the days of storage in plastic bags, when the stack of clay had to be kept damp under wet sacks, it was often not practical to sour it for more than a few weeks.

Sunpan. A shallow flat tank where the liquid slip is left to dry by evaporation, until it becomes firm enough to be worked.

Tudor greenware. A type of pottery produced in many potteries in west Surrey and around Cheam from the 14th century until well into the 16th century. The pale buff coloured clay of the pots was partially covered with a copper oxide stained lead glaze.

Wareboards. The boards or planks of wood onto which the freshly thrown ware would be put, also known as potboards. Once the board had been filled with a row of pots, it would be carried to racking, and replaced with another.

Wasters. Pots too warped or split by the firing, or otherwise unacceptable for sale.

Wheel-head. The disc of wood or metal on which the pots are thrown.

White salt-glazed pottery. Intricately moulded stoneware produced in Staffordshire in the 18th century.

Wicket. The temporary door into the kiln chamber. Dry-set bricks are built up to fill the space and then sealed on the outside with 'clamming', a mixture of sandy, refractory clay and water.

Bibliography

Books

Algar, D. & Light, A. & Copland-Griffiths, P. *Verwood and District Potteries; A Dorset Industry* (The Verwood and District Potteries Trust, 1979)

Anderson, J. *Making Pottery* (Smith Settle Ltd., 1998)

Artigas, J.L. *Spanish Folk Ceramics* (Editorial Blume, 1970)

Bebb, L. *Welsh Pottery* (Shire Publications Ltd., 1997)

Bonser, F. & Mossman, L. *Industrial Arts for Elementary Schools* (Macmillan, 1924)

Bourne (Sturt), G. *William Smith, Potter and Farmer 1790–1858* (Chatto & Windus, 1920)

Brannam, P. *A Family Business* (P. Brannam, 1982)

Brears, P. *A Collectors Book of English Country Pottery* (David & Charles, 1974)

Brears, P. *The English Country Pottery* (David & Charles, 1971)

Cardew, M. *A Pioneer Potter* (Collins, 1988)

Coleman-Smith, R. & Pearson, T. *Excavations in the Donyatt Potteries* (Phillimore, 1988)

Copland-Griffiths, P. *Discover Dorset; Pottery* (The Dovecote Press, 1998)

Davey, P. *Buckley Pottery* (Buckley Clay Industries Research Committee, 1975)

Davey, P. *Recent Fieldwork in the Buckley Potteries* (Post Medieval Archaeology, 1975)

Dobson, E. *A Rudimentary Treatise on the Manufacture of Bricks and Tiles , 1850* (Journal of Ceramic History, 1971)

Fishley-Holland, W. *Fifty Years A Potter*, (Pottery Quarterly, 1958)

Graham, M. *Cup and Saucer Land* (Madgwick Houlston & Co. Ltd., 1919)

Grant, A. *North Devon Pottery: The 17th Century* (University of Exeter, 1983)

Hartley, D. *Made in England* (Eyre Methuen, 1939 & 1977)

Keeling, J. *The Terracotta Gardener* (Headline, 1990)

Larder, D. *The Cabinet Cyclopaedia* (London, 1832)

Lawrence, H. *Yorkshire Pots and Potteries* (David & Charles, 1974)

Lewis, J. M. *The Ewenny Potteries* (National Museum of Wales, 1982)

Manwaring Baines, J. *Sussex Pottery* (Fisher Publications, 1980)

Messham, J.E. *The Buckley Potteries* (The Flintshire Miscellany, 1956)

Snell, J. *Wetheriggs Country Pottery, 19th-Century Industrial Monument* (Wetheriggs, 1980)

Strong, H.W. *Industries of North Devon* (David & Charles, 1889 & 1971)

Tyler, S. *Buckley Pottery* (Mostyn Art Gallery, 1983)

White, A. *Country Pottery from Burton in Lonsdale* (Lancaster City Museums, 1989)

Wheeler, R. *Winchcombe Pottery, The Cardew-Finch Tradition* (White Cockade Publishing, 1998)

William, E. *Medieval and Later Pottery in Wales. No. 2 (Breadovens)* (Welsh Medieval Pottery Research Group, 1979)

Wondrausch, M. *Mary Wondrausch on Slipware* (A & C Black, 1986)

Periodicals

Brears, P. *English Country Pottery (Yorkshire Museum Catalogue)*, (Yorkshire Philosophical Society, 1968)

Barker, D. *Slipware* (No. 297, 1993)

Bentley, J. *Buckley (The magazine of the Buckley Society)* (The Buckley Society 1970s–80s)

Cruikshank, G. *Scottish Pottery* (Shire Publications Ltd., No. 191, 1987)

Kendrick, T.P. *Pottery Quarterly* (Article: The Verwood Pottery, No. 24, 1959)

Mellor, M., Stebbing, N. & Rhodes, J. *Oxfordshire Potters*, (Oxfordshire Museum Services, No.13, 1980)

Stemp, S.W. *Pottery Quarterly* (Isaac Button of Soil Hill Pottery, No. 29, 1963)

Watkins, C.M. *Smithsonian (U.S.N.M.) Bulletin* (North Devon Pottery and its Export To America in the 17th Century, No. 225, 1960)

Films

Isaac Button, Country Potter (1965. Available from John Anderson, East View, The Green, Long Melford, Sudbury, Suffolk CO10 9DU)

Index